D1475827

GLOBAL
EXTREMISM
AND
TERRORISM

THE WORLD IN FOCUS

THE AMERICAN EMPIRE

DEMOCRACY IN THE MIDDLE EAST

GLOBAL EXTREMISM
AND TERRORISM

THE WORLD
IN FOCUS

GLOBAL
EXTREMISM
AND
TERRORISM

JOHN C. DAVENPORT, SERIES EDITOR

CHELSEA HOUSE
PUBLISHERS

An imprint of Infobase Publishing

Global Extremism and Terrorism

Copyright © 2007 by Infobase Publishing

All rights reserved. No part of this book may be reproduced or utilized in any form or by any means, electronic or mechanical, including photocopying, recording, or by any information storage or retrieval systems, without permission in writing from the publisher. For information, contact:

Chelsea House
An imprint of Infobase Publishing
132 West 31st Street
New York NY 10001

Library of Congress Cataloging-in-Publication Data
Global extremism and terrorism / [edited by] John C. Davenport.
     p.   cm. — (The World in focus)
   Includes bibliographical references and index.
   ISBN-13: 978-0-7910-9279-8 (hardcover)
   ISBN-10: 0-7910-9279-8 (hardcover)
1. Terrorism. I. Davenport, John, 1960-   II. Title. III. Series.
   HV6431.G555   2007
   363.325—dc22   2007004212

Chelsea House books are available at special discounts when purchased in bulk quantities for businesses, associations, institutions, or sales promotions. Please call our Special Sales Department in New York at (212) 967-8800 or (800) 322-8755.

You can find Chelsea House on the World Wide Web at
http://www.chelseahouse.com.

Text design by James Scotto-Lavino
Cover design by Takeshi Takahashi

Printed in the United States of America

Bang KT 10 9 8 7 6 5 4 3 2 1

This book is printed on acid-free paper.

All links and Web addresses were checked and verified to be correct at the time of publication. Because of the dynamic nature of the Web, some addresses and links may have changed since publication and may no longer be valid.

Contents Overview

Detailed Table of Contents

Introduction

⟨⟨⟨⟨⟩⟩⟩⟩

The swirl of twenty-first century current events can easily become overwhelming. With unprecedented speed, developments unfold, trends emerge, and crises arise. Every day, there seems to be more information demanding attention. Casual and expert observers alike carry a heavier burden of understanding, a weight made greater by the myriad interpretations of what takes place around the globe on a daily basis. Competing viewpoints crowd the marketplace of opinion; varying analyses of the latest issues vie for audiences and legitimacy. The resulting image of the modern world is thus blurred by abstraction and bias. People today, in short, have more difficulty than ever before in gaining a clear picture of what is going on around them. The challenge facing everyone, then, is to bring the world into focus.

This challenge is taken up in this series, a collection of three volumes that examine some of the most pressing and significant topics at the dawn of the new millennium. Each book plunges the reader into the disputes and debates that surround their subjects, assembling articles and excerpts from a variety of sources, including major books, the internet, and prestigious scholarly journals. Sifting through the various arguments and prescriptions offered by policy advocates, experts, and government agencies, *The World in Focus* examines three specific topic areas: Middle East democracy, American imperialism, and terrorism. The series explores each area in depth, then proceeds to lay out the many options for dealing with the problems associated with them. The arduous tasks of initiating democratic reform within Arab-Muslim society and politics, adapting to the reality of American hegemony, and combating extremism and terror are looked at in detail.

Throughout the volumes, multiple perspectives are reviewed, and a representative sample of contemporary thinking is offered. Authors expressing optimism concerning the chances for democratic change in the Middle East, for example, are coupled with those with more pessimistic outlooks. Supporters of the American assertion of imperial power are paired with its opponents. Writers who differ on the extent of the danger posed by global extremism, and the possible ways to counter it, are placed side by side. The reader will notice many voices in these three books, some more controversial than others. It is hoped that from this collection of analyses and interpretations, a deeper knowledge will be gained that might lead to better decision-making in the future.

DEMOCRACY IN THE MIDDLE EAST

There is perhaps no better place to start this process than the volatile Middle East. Plagued by a history of sectarian violence, repression, and colonialism, political evolution has been a bloody business for the Middle East in the past. Wars, assassination, and intrigue have often been the tools of choice among men and movements seeking to reshape the contours of power throughout a vast region that stretches from Africa to Asia. These struggles take place in an atmosphere charged further by the confluence of politics and Islam, a religion that shapes the lives of over one billion people.

Unsettled for centuries, the Middle East today serves as an arena for a monumental struggle between contesting political philosophies and systems. Traditional forms of autocracy and authoritarianism wrestle for dominance with newly imported strains of democracy. History favors the autocratic and authoritarian regimes that typify the Middle Eastern political landscape, but democracy is building momentum and gaining adherents, all the while being scrutinized for conformity to regional standards. Democracy is attractive to many people, but it must bear up under the strain of proving itself compatible with conservative social and religious norms. Some experts doubt democracy's chances for survival for these reasons; others are more hopeful. All of them, wary of making predictions, are guarded in their assessments.

Democracy in the Middle East presents their arguments and evaluations. It considers the prospects for democratic reform in a region notorious for tyranny, corruption, and inequity. The book's contributors weigh the odds that democratic institutions and political habits of thought can flourish there. Their essays and excerpts look at topics ranging from women's rights to the phenomenon of Muslim democracy. Each outlines and explains the powerful forces for both change and continuity in the Middle East and draws a conclusion as to whether or not democracy can flourish. The volume seeks to answer an important question: is there reason to hope that democracy might ever take root in such a troubled area?

THE AMERICAN EMPIRE

If so, the United States will almost certainly play a crucial role in its establishment. The United States has been and continues to be the most active agent for democratization in the Middle East. As a promoter of democracy, at least in theory, it is unsurpassed. But the American effort to export its political ideas and traditions is not limited to one region. The United States, in fact, is energetically working to reshape large parts of the world in its own image and create a universal political order that is liberal, democratic, secular, and built upon a solid foundation of consumer capitalism. The preferred tools for this job are cultural: movies, music, food, and fashion—but more muscular ones such as public diplomacy and even war are seen as equally valid and often more appropriate. The United States, put simply, has a vision of the world's future that is colored red, white, and blue.

Although viewed as benign or even benevolent by most Americans, many people in other countries wonder why the United States works so diligently to export its beliefs, customs, practices, and lifestyles overseas. They question American motivations and intentions. Perhaps, it is thought, American actions signal a commitment to a better, freer future for everyone. On the other hand, they very well could indicate an insatiable imperial hunger for domination. Is the United States seeking to become a global hegemon? Or is it already a de facto imperial state, an empire in everything but name? What does all this mean for the rest of the humanity?

The American Empire studies these questions and tries to determine whether and to what extent the United States is an empire, what kind it is, and how enduring it will be. The articles and excerpts generally presume America's imperial status, then move on to consider the costs and benefits of such a position. They also seek to place the United States on the continuum of historical empires and come to a conclusion regarding whether the American empire might succeed where so many others have failed.

GLOBAL EXTREMISM AND TERRORISM

Regardless of America's imperial future, its current degree of influence worldwide often generates substantial fear and resentment. Coupled with its championing of Western-style democracy, America's assertiveness creates enemies. For many ethnic and religious groups, the United States' expressions of power evoke memories of European colonialism, exploitation, and oppression. Americans appear, to their eyes, to be just another band of arrogant foreigners bent on controlling the planet, its people, and its resources.

Not surprisingly, forces have emerged in resistance to American goals and objectives. Around the world, movements have sprung up in opposition to everything viewed as either a Western or specifically American import. Usually these movements employ peaceful means of protest. Sometimes, however, driven by local or regional impulses, they devolve into extremism and begin advocating more aggressive forms of reaction, up to and including violence. On occasion, movements transition from words to deeds; they transform themselves into terrorist cells and even transnational terrorist organizations. They adopt violence as both a strategy and tactic for advancing their anti-Western, anti-American agendas. Bombings, kidnappings, assassinations, and executions soon follow.

The third volume in *The World in Focus* surveys the dark and treacherous landscape of terrorism. *Global Extremism and Terrorism* seeks to define, describe, and illuminate the people who have chosen murder and mayhem as weapons in a war against belief systems and ways of life they view as evil. The book leads its readers into a violent netherworld where individuals and groups openly embrace destruction as a vehicle for change. The contributors look at who terrorists are and why they do the things they do. The often twisted motivations and justifications for destruction and the taking of innocent lives are dissected in search of some form of underlying logic. The chosen means of violence, ranging from piracy to suicide bombings, are explored and explained so that the audience can appreciate just how devastating the realization of terrorist plans can be. Lastly, *Global Extremism and Terrorism* weighs the options for counter-terrorist activity. How best to fight terrorism, and end its scourge, is a question for which tentative answers are offered. The world promises to become a far more dangerous place unless the agents of terror and their tools are better understood.

Taken together, the three books in this series sharpen the outlines of the modern world. They help lift the veil of confusion that too often obscures the popular views of current events, and reveal the inner structures of the issues that dominate today's headlines. A degree of blurriness will no doubt persist despite the best efforts of scholars and experts like those represented in *Democracy in the Middle East*, *The American Empire*, and *Global Extremism and Terrorism*. Nevertheless, each book does its part to clarify key global developments and, through close examination, bring them and the world into focus.

John C. Davenport
Series Editor

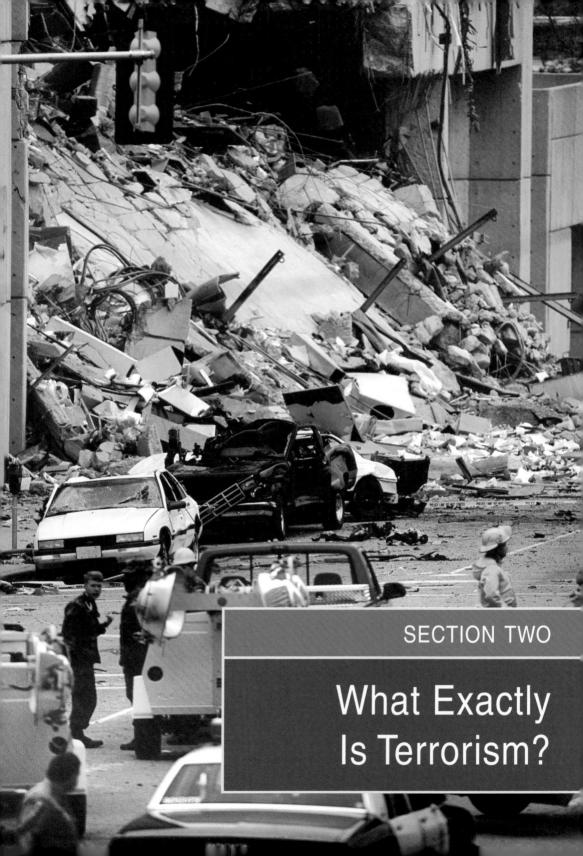

SECTION TWO

What Exactly Is Terrorism?

One hundred years ago, terrorism could be defined simply as a form of violence perpetrated by fringe groups seeking radical political change. These groups tended to be small, and their operations were always quite limited. Terrorist targets, at that time, were almost exclusively political leaders or members of the social elite. Assassination was normally the objective. Not only were the missions relatively straight-forward, so were the means of accomplishing them. The weapons and tactics used by early terrorists were absurdly crude by today's standards—revolvers, daggers, and hand-thrown bombs. It is true that the rhetoric of violence employed by armed radicals in the late nineteenth and early twentieth centuries was every bit as fiery as that used by their modern counterparts. But the destructive potential of the old-time extremists pales by comparison.

When considering terrorist organizations such as al Qaeda and men such as Osama bin Laden, more than one observer has agreed with Isaac Cronin that the terrorism of yesteryear "was certainly more smoke than fire."* Despite all the talk of revolution, overthrow, and anarchy, between 1870 and 1917, fewer than 50 deaths in all of Europe and North America could be attributed directly to terrorist action.

Matters now are very different. The cruel calculus of terrorism has changed dramatically during the course of the last century. The destructive arsenal available to extremists has grown in size, sophistication, and lethality. Terrorist groups are larger and operate increasingly on a global scale. Perhaps most disturbing, their stated goals have become broader and more general, to the point of becoming frustratingly vague. As Walter Laqueur points out in this 1996 article, terrorism has evolved into a truly postmodern phenomenon; it is dizzying in its complexity, confounding in its ends, and nearly impenetrable in its logic. Taken together, these qualities have made it more dangerous than ever.

NOTES

* Isaac Cronin, *Confronting Fear: A History of Terrorism* (New York: Thunder's Mouth Press, 2002), 2.

Postmodern Terrorism
WALTER LAQUEUR

NEW RULES FOR AN OLD GAME

As the nineteenth century ended, it seemed no one was safe from terrorist attack. In 1894 an Italian anarchist assassinated French President Sadi Carnot. In 1897 anarchists fatally stabbed Empress Elizabeth of Austria and killed Antonio Cánovas, the Spanish prime minister. In 1900 Umberto I, the Italian king, fell in yet another anarchist attack; in 1901 an American anarchist killed William McKinley, president of the United States. Terrorism became the leading preoccupation of politicians, police chiefs, journalists, and writers from Dostoevsky to Henry James. If in the year 1900 the leaders of the main industrial powers had assembled, most of them would have insisted on giving terrorism top priority on their agenda, as President Clinton did at the Group of Seven meeting after the June bombing of the U.S. military compound in Dhahran, Saudi Arabia.

From this perspective the recent upsurge of terrorist activity is not particularly threatening. According to the State Department's annual report on the subject, fewer people died last year in incidents of international terrorism (165) than the year before (314). Such figures, however, are almost meaningless, because of both the incidents they disregard and those they count. Current definitions of terrorism fail to capture the magnitude of the problem worldwide.

Terrorism has been defined as the substate application of violence or threatened violence intended to sow panic in a society, to weaken or even overthrow the incumbents, and to bring about political change. It shades on occasion into guerrilla warfare (although unlike guerrillas, terrorists are unable or unwilling to take or hold territory) and even a substitute for war between states. In its long history terrorism has appeared in many guises; today society faces not one terrorism but many terrorisms.

Since 1900, terrorists' motivation, strategy, and weapons have changed to some extent. The anarchists and the left-wing terrorist groups that succeeded them, down through the Red Armies that operated in Germany, Italy, and Japan in the 1970s, have vanished; if anything, the initiative has passed to the extreme right. Most international and domestic terrorism these days, however, is neither left nor right, but ethnic-separatist in inspiration. Ethnic terrorists have more staying power than ideologically motivated ones, since they draw on a larger reservoir of public support.

The greatest change in recent decades is that terrorism is by no means militants' only strategy. The many-branched Muslim Brotherhood, the Palestinian Hamas, the Irish Republican Army (IRA), the Kurdish extremists in Turkey and Iraq, the Tamil Tigers of Sri Lanka, the Basque Homeland and Liberty (ETA) movement in Spain, and many other groups that have sprung up in this century have had political as well as terrorist wings from the beginning. The political arm provides social services and education, runs businesses, and contests elections, while the "military wing" engages in ambushes and assassinations. Such division of labor has advantages: the political leadership can publicly disassociate itself when the terrorists commit a particularly outrageous act or something goes wrong. The claimed lack of control can be quite real because the armed wing tends to become independent; the men and women with the guns and bombs often lose sight of the movement's wider aims and may end up doing more harm than good.

Terrorist operations have also changed somewhat. Airline hijackings have become rare, since hijacked planes cannot stay in the air forever and few countries today are willing to let them land, thereby incurring the stigma of openly supporting terrorism. Terrorists, too, saw diminishing returns on hijackings. The trend now seems to be away from attacking specific targets like the other side's officials and toward more indiscriminate killing. Furthermore, the dividing line between urban terrorism and other tactics has become less distinct, while the line between politically motivated terrorism and the operation of national and international crime syndicates is often impossible for outsiders to discern in the former Soviet Union, Latin America, and other parts of the world. But there is one fundamental difference between international crime and terrorism: mafias have no interest in overthrowing the government and decisively weakening society; in fact, they have a vested interest in a prosperous economy.

Misapprehensions, not only semantic, surround the various forms of political violence. A terrorist is not a guerrilla, strictly speaking. There are no longer any guerrillas, engaging in Maoist-style liberation of territories that become the base of a counter-society and a regular army fighting the central government—except perhaps in remote places like Afghanistan, the Philippines, and Sri Lanka. The term "guerrilla" has had a long life partly because terrorists prefer the label, for its more positive connotations. It also persists because governments and media in other countries do not wish to offend terrorists by calling them terrorists. The French and British press would not dream of referring to their countries' native terrorists by any other name but call terrorists in other nations militants, activists, national liberation fighters, or even "gun persons."

The belief has gained ground that terrorist missions by volunteers bent on committing suicide constitute a radical new departure, dangerous because they are impossible to prevent. But that is a myth, like the many others in which terrorism has always been shrouded. The bomber willing and indeed eager to blow himself up has appeared in all eras and cultural traditions, espousing politics ranging from the leftism of the Baader-Meinhof Gang in 1970s Germany to rightist extremism. When the Japanese military wanted kamikaze pilots at the end of World War II, thousands of volunteers rushed to offer themselves. The young Arab bombers on Jerusalem buses looking to be rewarded by the virgins in Paradise are a link in an old chain.

State-sponsored terrorism has not disappeared. Terrorists can no longer count on the Soviet Union and its Eastern European allies, but some Middle Eastern and North African countries still provide support. Tehran and Tripoli, however, are less eager to argue that they have a divine right to engage in terrorist operations outside their borders; the 1986 U.S. air strike against Libya and the various boycotts against Libya and Iran had an effect. No government today boasts about surrogate warfare it instigates and backs.

On the other hand, Sudan, without fanfare, has become for terrorists what the Barbary Coast was for pirates of another age: a safe haven. Politically isolated and presiding over a disastrous economy, the military government in Khartoum, backed by Muslim leaders, believes that no one wants to become involved in Sudan and thus it can get away with lending support to terrorists from many nations. Such confidence is justified so long as terrorism is only a nuisance. But if it becomes more than that, the rules of the game change, and both terrorists and their protectors come under great pressure.

OPPORTUNITIES IN TERRORISM

History shows that terrorism more often than not has little political impact, and that when it has an effect it is often the opposite of the one desired. Terrorism in the 1980s and 1990s is no exception. The 1991 assassination of Rajiv Gandhi as he campaigned to retake the prime ministership neither hastened nor inhibited the decline of India's Congress Party. Hamas' and Hezbollah's stepped-up terrorism in Israel undoubtedly influenced the outcome of Israeli elections in May, but while it achieved its immediate objective of setting back the peace process on which Palestine Authority President Yasir Arafat has gambled his future, is a hard-line Likud government really in these groups' interests? On the other side, Yigal Amir, the right-wing orthodox Jewish student who assassinated

Prime Minister Yitzhak Rabin [in November 1995] because he disapproved of the peace agreement with the Palestinians, might well have helped elect Rabin's dovish second-in-command, Shimon Peres, to a full term had the Muslim terrorists not made Israeli security an issue again.

Terrorists caused disruption and destabilization in other parts of the world, such as Sri Lanka, where economic decline has accompanied the war between the government and the Tamil Tigers. But in Israel and in Spain, where Basque extremists have been staging attacks for decades, terrorism has had no effect on the economy. Even in Algeria, where terrorism has exacted the highest toll in human lives, Muslim extremists have made little headway since 1992–93, when many predicted the demise of the unpopular military regime.

Some argue that terrorism must be effective because certain terrorist leaders have become president or prime minister of their country. In those cases, however, the terrorists had first forsworn violence and adjusted to the political process. Finally, the common wisdom holds that terrorism can spark a war or, at least, prevent peace. That is true, but only where there is much inflammable material: as in Sarajevo in 1914, so in the Middle East and elsewhere today. Nor can one ever say with certainty that the conflagration would not have occurred sooner or later in any case.

Nevertheless, terrorism's prospects, often overrated by the media, the public, and some politicians, are improving as its destructive potential increases. This has to do both with the rise of groups and individuals that practice or might take up terrorism and with the weapons available to them. The past few decades have witnessed the birth of dozens of aggressive movements espousing varieties of nationalism, religious fundamentalism, fascism, and apocalyptic millenarianism, from Hindu nationalists in India to neofascists in Europe and the developing world to the Branch Davidian cult of Waco, Texas. The earlier fascists believed in military aggression and engaged in a huge military buildup, but such a strategy has become too expensive even for superpowers. Now, mail-order catalogs tempt militants with readily available, far cheaper, unconventional as well as conventional weapons—the poor man's nuclear bomb, Iranian President Ali Akbar Hashemi Rafsanjani called them.

In addition to nuclear arms, the weapons of mass destruction include biological agents and man-made chemical compounds that attack the nervous system, skin, or blood. Governments have engaged in the production of chemical weapons for almost a century and in the production of nuclear and biological weapons for many decades, during which time proliferation has been continuous and access ever easier.[1] The means of delivery— ballistic missiles, cruise missiles, and aerosols—have also become far more effective. While in the past missiles were deployed only in wars between states, recently they have played a role in civil wars in Afghanistan and Yemen. Use by terrorist groups would be but one step further.

Until the 1970s most observers believed that stolen nuclear material constituted the greatest threat in the escalation of terrorist weapons, but many now think the danger could lie elsewhere. An April 1996 Defense Department report says that "most terrorist groups do not have the financial and technical resources to acquire nuclear weapons but could gather materials to make radiological dispersion devices and some biological and chemical agents." Some groups have state sponsors that possess or can obtain weapons of the latter three types. Terrorist groups themselves have investigated the use of poisons since the nineteenth century. The Aum Shinrikyo cult staged a poison gas attack in March 1995 in the Tokyo subway; exposure to the nerve gas sarin killed ten people and injured 5,000. Other, more amateurish attempts in the United States and abroad to experiment with chemical substances and biological agents for use in terrorism have involved the toxin that causes botulism, the poisonous protein rycin (twice), sarin (twice), bubonic plague bacteria, typhoid bacteria, hydrogen cyanide, VX (another nerve gas), and possibly the Ebola virus.

TO USE OR NOT TO USE?

If terrorists have used chemical weapons only once and nuclear material never, to some extent the reasons are technical. The scientific literature is replete with the technical problems inherent in the production, manufacture, storage, and delivery of each of the three classes of unconventional weapons.

The manufacture of nuclear weapons is not that simple, nor is delivery to their target. Nuclear material, of which a limited supply exists, is monitored by the U.N.-affiliated International Atomic Energy Agency. Only governments can legally procure it, so that even in this age of proliferation investigators could trace those abetting nuclear terrorists without great difficulty. Monitoring can overlook a more primitive nuclear weapon: nonfissile but radioactive nuclear material. Iranian agents in Turkey, Kazakhstan, and elsewhere are known to have tried to buy such material originating in the former Soviet Union.

Chemical agents are much easier to produce or obtain but not so easy to keep safely in stable condition, and their dispersal depends largely on climatic factors. The terrorists behind last year's attack in Tokyo chose a convenient target where crowds of people gather, but their sarin was apparently dilute. The biological agents are far and away the most dangerous: they could kill hundreds of thousands where chemicals might kill only thousands. They are relatively easy to procure, but storage and dispersal are even trickier than for nerve gases. The risk of contamination for the people handling them is high, and many of the most lethal bacteria and spores do not survive well outside the laboratory. Aum Shinrikyo reportedly released anthrax bacteria—among the most toxic agents known—on two occasions from a building in Tokyo without harming anyone.

Given the technical difficulties, terrorists are probably less likely to use nuclear devices than chemical weapons, and least likely to attempt to use biological weapons. But difficulties could be overcome, and the choice of unconventional weapons will in the end come down to the specialties of the terrorists and their access to deadly substances.

The political arguments for shunning unconventional weapons are equally weighty. The risk of detection and subsequent severe retaliation or punishment is great, and while this may not deter terrorists it may put off their sponsors and suppliers. Terrorists eager to use weapons of mass destruction may alienate at least some supporters, not so much because the dissenters hate the enemy less or have greater moral qualms but because they think the use of such violence counterproductive. Unconventional weapon strikes could render whole regions uninhabitable for long periods. Use of biological arms poses the additional risk of an uncontrollable epidemic. And while terrorism seems to be tending toward more indiscriminate killing and mayhem, terrorists may draw the line at weapons of super-violence likely to harm both foes and large numbers of relatives and friends—say, Kurds in Turkey, Tamils in Sri Lanka, or Arabs in Israel.

Furthermore, traditional terrorism rests on the heroic gesture, on the willingness to sacrifice one's own life as proof of one's idealism. Obviously there is not much heroism in spreading botulism or anthrax. Since most terrorist groups are as interested in publicity as in violence, and as publicity for a mass poisoning or nuclear bombing would be far more unfavorable than for a focused conventional attack, only terrorists who do not care about publicity will even consider the applications of unconventional weapons.

Broadly speaking, terrorists will not engage in overkill if their traditional weapons—the submachine gun and the conventional bomb—are sufficient to continue the struggle and achieve their aims. But the decision to use terrorist violence is not always a rational one; if it were, there would be much less terrorism, since terrorist activity seldom achieves its aims. What if, after years of armed struggle and the loss of many of their militants, terrorist groups see no progress? Despair could lead to giving up the armed struggle, or to suicide. But it might also lead to a last desperate attempt to defeat the hated enemy by arms not tried before. As one of Racine's heroes said of himself, their "only hope lies in their despair."

APOCALYPSE SOON

Terrorist groups traditionally contain strong quasi-religious, fanatical elements, for only total certainty of belief (or total moral relativism) provides justification for taking lives. That element was strong among the prerevolutionary Russian terrorists and the Romanian fascists of the Iron Guard in the 1930s, as it is among today's Tamil Tigers. Fanatical Muslims consider the killing of the enemies of God a religious commandment, and believe that the secularists at home as well as the State of Israel will be annihilated because it is Allah's will. Aum Shinrikyo doctrine held that murder could help both victim and murderer to salvation. Sectarian fanaticism has surged during the past decade, and in general, the smaller the group, the more fanatical.

As humankind approaches the end of the second millennium of the Christian era, apocalyptic movements are on the rise. The belief in the impending end of the world is probably as old as history, but for reasons not entirely clear, sects and movements preaching the end of the world gain influence toward the end of a century, and all the more at the close of a millennium. Most of the preachers of doom do not advocate violence, and some even herald a renaissance, the birth of a new kind of man and woman. Others, however, believe that the sooner the reign of the Antichrist is established, the sooner this corrupt world will be destroyed and the new heaven and earth foreseen by St. John in the Book of Revelation, Nostradamus, and a host of other prophets will be realized.[2]

Extremist millenarians would like to give history a push, helping create world-ending havoc replete with universal war, famine, pestilence, and other scourges. It is possible that members of certain Christian and Jewish sects that believe in Armageddon or Gog and Magog or the Muslims and Buddhists who harbor related extreme beliefs could attempt to play out a doomsday scenario. A small group of Israeli extremists, for instance, firmly believes that blowing up Temple Mount in Jerusalem would bring about a final (religious) war and the beginning of redemption with the coming of the Kingdom of God. The visions of Shoko Asahara, the charismatic leader of Aum Shinrikyo, grew increasingly apocalyptic, and David Koresh proclaimed the Last Day's arrival in the Branch Davidians' 1994 confrontation with Bureau of Alcohol, Tobacco, and Firearms agents.

Those who subscribe to such beliefs number in the hundreds of thousands and perhaps millions. They have their own subcultures, produce books and CDs by the thousands, and build temples and communities of whose existence most of their contemporaries are unaware. They have substantial financial means at their disposal. Although the more extreme apocalyptic groups are potentially terrorist, intelligence services have generally overlooked their activities; hence the shock over the subway attack in Tokyo and Rabin's assassination, to name but two recent events.

Apocalyptic elements crop up in contemporary intellectual fashions and extremist politics as well. For instance, extreme environmentalists, particularly the so-called restoration ecologists, believe that environmental disasters will destroy civilization as we know it—no loss, in their view—and regard the vast majority of human beings as expendable. From such beliefs and values it is not a large step to engaging in acts of terrorism to expedite the process. If the eradication of smallpox upset ecosystems, why not restore the balance by bringing back the virus? The motto of *Chaos International*, one of many journals in this field, is a quotation from Hassan I Sabbah, the master of the Assassins, a medieval sect whose members killed Crusaders and others in a "religious" ecstasy; everything is permitted, the master says. The premodern world and postmodernism meet at this point.

FUTURE SHOCK

Scanning the contemporary scene, one encounters a bewildering multiplicity of terrorist and potentially terrorist groups and sects. The practitioners of terrorism as we have known it to this point were nationalists and anarchists, extremists of the left and the right. But the new age has brought new inspiration for the users of violence along with the old.

In the past, terrorism was almost always the province of groups of militants that had the backing of political forces like the Irish and Russian social revolutionary movements of 1900. In the future, terrorists will be individuals or like-minded people working in very small groups, on the pattern of the technology-hating Unabomber, who apparently worked alone sending out parcel bombs over two decades, or the perpetrators of the 1995 bombing of the federal building in Oklahoma City. An individual may possess the technical competence to steal, buy, or manufacture the weapons he or she needs for a terrorist purpose; he or she may or may not require help from one or two others in delivering these weapons to the designated target. The ideologies such individuals and mini-groups espouse are likely to be even more aberrant than those of larger groups.

And terrorists working alone or in very small groups will be more difficult to detect unless they make a major mistake or are discovered by accident.

Thus at one end of the scale, the lone terrorist has appeared, and at the other, state-sponsored terrorism is quietly flourishing in these days when wars of aggression have become too expensive and too risky. As the century draws to a close, terrorism is becoming the substitute for the great wars of the 1800s and early 1900s.

Proliferation of the weapons of mass destruction does not mean that most terrorist groups are likely to use them in the foreseeable future, but some almost certainly will, in spite of all the reasons militating against it. Governments, however ruthless, ambitious, and ideologically extreme, will be reluctant to pass on unconventional weapons to terrorist groups over which they cannot have full control; the governments may be tempted to use such arms themselves in a first strike, but it is more probable that they would employ them in blackmail than in actual warfare. Individuals and small groups, however, will not be bound by the constraints that hold back even the most reckless government.

Society has also become vulnerable to a new kind of terrorism, in which the destructive power of both the individual terrorist and terrorism as a tactic are infinitely greater. Earlier terrorists could kill kings or high officials, but others only too eager to inherit their mantle quickly stepped in. The advanced societies of today are more dependent every day on the electronic storage, retrieval, analysis, and transmission of information. Defense, the police, banking, trade, transportation, scientific work, and a large percentage of the government's and the private sector's transactions are on-line. That exposes enormous vital areas of national life to mischief or sabotage by any computer hacker, and concerted sabotage could render a country unable to function. Hence the growing speculation about infoterrorism and cyberwarfare.

An unnamed U.S. intelligence official has boasted that with $1 billion and 20 capable hackers, he could shut down America. What he could achieve, a terrorist could too. There is little secrecy in the wired society, and protective measures have proved of limited value: teenage hackers have penetrated highly secret systems in every field. The possibilities for creating chaos are almost unlimited even now, and vulnerability will almost certainly increase. Terrorists' targets will change: Why assassinate a politician or indiscriminately kill people when an attack on electronic switching will produce far more dramatic and lasting results? The switch at the Culpeper, Virginia, headquarters of the Federal Reserve's electronic network, which handles all federal funds and transactions, would be an obvious place to hit. If the new terrorism directs its energies toward information warfare, its destructive power will be exponentially greater than any it wielded in the past—greater even than it would be with biological and chemical weapons.

Still, the vulnerability of states and societies will be of less interest to terrorists than to ordinary criminals and organized crime, disgruntled employees of big corporations, and, of course, spies and hostile governments. Electronic thieves, whether engaged in credit card fraud or industrial espionage, are part of the system, using it rather than destroying it; its destruction would cost them their livelihood. Politically motivated terrorist groups, above all separatists bent on establishing states of their own, have limited aims. The Kurdish Workers Party, the IRA, the Basque ETA, and the Tamil Tigers want to weaken their enemies and compel them to make far-reaching concessions, but they cannot realistically hope to destroy them. It is also possible, however, that terrorist groups on the verge of defeat or acting on apocalyptic visions may not hesitate to apply all destructive means at their disposal.

All that leads well beyond terrorism as we have known it. New definitions and new terms may have to be developed for new realities, and intelligence services and policymakers must learn to discern the significant differences among terrorists' motivations, approaches, and aims. The Bible says that when the Old Testament hero Samson brought down the temple, burying himself along with the Philistines in the ruins, "the dead which he slew at his death were more than he slew in his life." The Samsons of a society have been relatively few in all ages. But with the new technologies and the changed nature of the world in which they operate, a handful of angry Samsons and disciples of apocalypse would suffice to cause havoc. Chances are that of 100 attempts at terrorist superviolence, 99 would fail. But the single successful one could claim many more victims, do more material damage, and unleash far greater panic than anything the world has yet experienced.

NOTES

1. Science fiction writers produced chemical weapons even earlier. In Jules Verne's *The Begum's Fortune*, a (German) scientist aims to wipe out the 250,000 inhabitants of (French) Franceville with one grenade of what he calls carbon acid gas, shot from a supergun.

2. According to Nostradamus, a "great King of terror" will come from heaven in July 1999. Millenarians face a problem when it comes to fixing the date; the Gospel of St. Matthew says that "no one knows the day and the hour, not even the angels in heaven." As the year 1000 approached, educated people were fully aware that the Christian cal-

endar was inexact and could not be corrected—hence the assumption that the world could end almost anytime between 960 and 1040. For a comparative review of apocalyptic influences at the end of the nineteenth and the twentieth centuries, see Walter Laqueur, "Fin de Siècle—Once More with Feeling," *Journal of Contemporary History*, January 1996, pp. 5–47.

Reprinted by permission of FOREIGN AFFAIRS, (September/October 1996). Copyright 2007 by the Council on Foreign Relations, Inc.

An early al Qaeda training manual urged the group's operatives to maintain a protocol of strict secrecy. Absolute security was required, the manual said, "even with the closest people, for deceiving the enemy is not easy."* The task of ferreting out individual terrorists and terrorist cells, the al Qaeda book acknowledged, would be less difficult in direct proportion to the number of people who had access to critical pieces of information. One bit of intelligence here could be connected to others there, allowing a thread to be spun that just might weave together an entire terrorist community. An entire terror network could be undermined by linking its members together one at a time, based on the secrets each one could be coaxed into divulging.

The crucial importance of utter secrecy, therefore, is apparent, and helps explain one of the most troubling postmodern traits of global terrorism—the seemingly invisible bonds between the terrorists themselves. Security concerns within terror groups have led to the appearance of what Jeremy Pressman, the author of the next article, calls the "leaderless resistance." Terrorism, according to this redefinition, cannot be understood as the work of traditional extremist organizations, complete with leaders, followers, and discernible lines of command, control, and communication. Instead, operatives, working alone or in tiny local cells, have acquired the capability to strike at will without reference to any centralized authority. Their capture, therefore, no longer carries the value it once did. Likewise, killing any one terrorist has little impact on the overall functioning of the group or groups they serve. If Pressman is correct, defeating a terrorism that has become leaderless will be an immensely tougher and bloodier job.

NOTES

* Al Qaeda Training Manual, Military Series, www.fas.org/irp/world/para/manualpart1_1.pdf (accessed December 7, 2006).

Leaderless Resistance: The Next Threat?
JEREMY PRESSMAN

After September 11, 2001, the United States focused not only on Al Qaeda in general but also on its base of operations: Afghanistan. The country's ruling Taliban regime had provided Al Qaeda with diplomatic cover, material support, and a secure location for training camps. The Bush administration concluded that a large part of confronting Al Qaeda was denying the international terrorist organization a home base and killing or capturing its leaders. "By destroying camps and disrupting communications," President George W. Bush told the nation on October 7, 2001, as the United States was launching its attack on Afghanistan, "we will make it more difficult for the terror network to train new recruits and coordinate their evil plans."

The war in Afghanistan dismantled major elements of Al Qaeda's base of operations in that country. Yet, even though now fragmented, with most remnants believed to be scattered in the mountains of Afghanistan and neighboring Pakistan, Al Qaeda remains a potent force. As the United States and its allies think through how best to confront the terrorist threat, a new question should focus the attention of those devising counterterrorism strategy: What if the next generation of Al Qaeda has neither a central leadership nor a territorial base? If a terrorist organization could find a model for operating without its own Afghanistan, it would pose a different and perhaps more difficult set of challenges for counterterrorist forces.

INSTRUCTIONS NOT INCLUDED

One model for organizations that seek to operate in a decentralized fashion is leaderless resistance, a form of non-organization long embraced by elements of the far right in the United States. It is similar to a cell structure, but with no guiding hand at the center that sets up the cells or monitors their progress; Peter Chalk, writing in *Jane's Intelligence Review*, has described it as "non-hierarchical," "unstructured," and "disaggregated."

Leaderless resistance assumes, first, that multiple individuals or clusters of people hold common views and are willing to act on those views in a confrontational or violent manner. They are willing to act in support of their views even though they have never met and may not be aware of others who share their views and are also prepared to act.

A second assumption is the existence of a catalyst, helping those with common views to make the move from thought to action. Each act of violence may spawn copycats; leaderless resistance depends on a demonstration effect. One act gets the ball rolling. Then others who have no material connection to the initial perpetrators, but who share their ideological commitments, follow with their own attacks. The terrorists are united in purpose but disconnected in implementation.

Leaderless resistance need not even be a conscious act. Terrorists may simply believe they act alone and need not have a sense of the non-organization of which they are implicitly a part. Isolated pinpricks nonetheless may cause damage to a government, system, or society under attack.

The absence of a central territorial home also follows from leaderless resistance. In a leaderless, individualized environment, there is no natural place for centralized training camps and overt national patrons.

LONE SNIPERS

Two cases, albeit drawn from outside the realm of international or Islamist terrorism, shed light on what the United States and others might face in the future. The two men who engaged in a series of sniper shootings in the Washington D.C. area in October 2002 and the Earth Liberation Front (ELF), a militant environmental group, illustrate the potential of leaderless resistance. Although ELF is not fully leaderless and the D.C. snipers probably lacked a clear political objective, these two domestic cases offer lessons about leadership and territoriality for both would-be international terrorists and their pursuers.

For three weeks last October, John Allen Muhammed and John Lee Malvo allegedly went on a shooting spree in metropolitan Washington. They operated alone, without any connection to other individuals or a larger organization, and moved across the United States by car and bus. Armed with a Bushmaster XM15 semi-automatic rifle, they killed ten people and wounded three in the Washington area alone, according to law enforcement officials. In all, they have been charged or suspected in 21 shootings in Alabama, the District of Columbia, Georgia, Louisiana, Maryland, Washington, and Virginia.

Had the snipers focused just on shooting and not on garnering attention or a bounty, police would have had a more difficult time tracking them down. Muhammed and Malvo were captured on October 24 only because they offered their pursuers a number of clues. They made two phone calls to police on October 17 and 18 that led to the discovery of Malvo's fingerprints in an older, unresolved matter; they tried unsuccessfully to contact authorities on a half-dozen other occasions. They left notes for police at least twice.

The D.C. snipers' motives are not certain, but they were probably not terrorists in the sense of using violence to spread fear in pursuit of a political objective. They may have wanted money (they asked for $10 million), sought revenge against Muhammed's second wife, who had custody of their children, or been driven by racist experiences during Muhammed's army days.

The tactics they used, however, could easily be adopted by an individual with a political agenda. With no territorial ties and no directions from above, they suggest a perfect if nefarious model for would-be terrorists. The snipers caused widespread fear and greatly disrupted daily life for hundreds of thousands of people. If, unlike the D.C. snipers, terrorist snipers offered no information to authorities that might lead to their own capture, they might be able to avoid capture for a much longer time. (The anthrax attacks in the United States in the fall of 2001 may be seen as another example of this kind of terrorism, although not knowing who carried out the attacks, or why, makes it difficult to draw any firm conclusions.)

ENVIRO-MILITANTS

The Earth Liberation Front offers a second illustrative case. ELF broke from the environmental group Earth First! in 1992 and began operating in the United States in 1997. According to its website (http://earth-liberationfront.com/about/), ELF seeks to "inflict economic damage on those profiting from the destruction and exploitation of the natural environment" and to "reveal and educate the public on the atrocities committed against the earth and all species that populate it." ELF has no known centralized territorial home within the United States.

ELF operations have included burning sports utility vehicles at a Los Angeles car dealership and torching luxury homes and an apartment complex on Long Island and in Detroit and San Diego. As of late 2003, the attacks had caused about $100 million damage and no deaths.

ELF's structure has been described by others as "anonymous cells," a "loose amalgam of environmental terrorists," and "more autonomous cells and individuals than actual groups." The front describes itself as non-hierarchical: "individuals involved control their own activities." No centralized organization or leadership ties the anonymous cells together. Likewise, there is no official "membership." ELF defines supporters not as people who belong but as those who have perpetrated acts consistent with ELF's philosophy: "Any direct action to halt the destruction of the environment and adhering to the strict nonviolence guidelines . . . can be considered an ELF action." In a similar vein, "There is no way to contact the ELF in your area. It is up to each committed person to take responsibility for stopping the exploitation of the natural world."

ELF is not purely leaderless, but it is, at a minimum, highly decentralized. While the group no longer has a public spokesperson, anonymous individuals run the North American Earth Liberation Front press office. Some reports have alleged that veteran ELF activists recruit individuals for the organization rather than relying solely on spontaneous destructive acts. Given that ELF also encompasses actions by unaffiliated individuals, it may be best to think of the group as combining both leaderless resistance and decentralized, autonomous cells.

LOW COST, LOW OVERHEAD

What can we learn from the sniper attacks and ELF? First, leaderless resisters may benefit from the work of other organized groups that share the same objectives but choose law-abiding or peaceful tactics of protest. ELF supporters may agree with supporters of the Nature Conservancy or the Sierra Club about the importance of environmental protection, but they are deeply divided with such establishment environmental organizations as to the best tactics to protect the environment. When other groups build environmental consciousness, it is a non-exclusive good that may also inform and motivate more radical individuals who choose to respond differently.

Second, terrorists do not require sophisticated technology and training to wreak havoc. In the fall of 2002, two men with a semi-automatic rifle and a 1990 Chevrolet Caprice were able to terrorize the capital city of the world's only superpower. Both the D.C. snipers and ELF serve as reminders that the goal of terrorists can be any form of terror, not just mass casualties. In the aftermath of the nearly 3,000 dead from 9-11, we may have lost our sense that terrorism is about spreading fear and, as a result of that fear, causing people to change their behavior or governments to change their policies. For this purpose, simple training and traditional weapons may suffice.

The absence of a base of operations could be crucial if centralized training were necessary for successful terrorism. The lack of a central leadership would be significant if a terrorist group's operations needed extensive coordination. If, however, operations are simple and low tech, the potential for minimally trained terrorists to be successful rises.

Third, leaderless resistance may make the penetration and exposure of terrorists more difficult. When so few people know whom the terrorists are, counterterrorism efforts become akin to finding the needle in the haystack. If one or two terrorists constitute the entire cell, there may be no others to lead officials to it. Counterterrorist operatives cannot pump other members for information because there are no other members. Granted, other factors might help expose isolated terrorists. In the absence of a central training camp, they may lack the intense indoctrination required for sustained commitment to the cause. Their morale may weaken over time. And with less training in operating covertly, they may also tend toward amateurishness in efforts to hide their activities. Jacob Sherman, an ELF activist now in prison, was turned in to the FBI by his father after Sherman, then 19 years old, "drove home reeking of gasoline the night three logging company trucks were attacked."

Fourth, leaderless resistance benefits from the role played by mass media. The media may convey the initial stories that enrage and activate the terrorist. Beyond motivation, a single, isolated terrorist attack widely reported might serve as a spark or example for others along the lines of copycat crimes. The media, in a sense, do the recruiting for the non-organization; perhaps one could think of the importance of outsourcing in leaderless resistance. Also, as is often alleged in major criminal probes, the terrorists may learn something about their adversary from the media. The D.C. snipers reportedly followed the news coverage of their shooting spree.

Finally, open societies make leaderless resistance much easier. Protection of civil liberties is the antithesis of the kind of police state required to survey citizens' activities and watch all potential terrorists. More important, the vulnerabilities of an open society are self-evident. The sophisticated planning needed to pull off the 9-11 attacks is misleading when contrasted with the D.C. snipers. Terrorists do not need to engage in elaborate target analysis and selection. The kinds of actions that will sow fear, if not cause mass panic, are both evident and common. Militants can easily find the soft spots in the world's liberal democratic states.

Many of these factors point in exactly the direction that may facilitate leaderless resistance: low-cost terrorism. By outsourcing organizational tasks to other nongovernmental actors or the media, by using simple weaponry and technology, by avoiding organizational expenses, and by taking advantage of self-evident target selection, terrorists of limited means and number can nonetheless be successful.

AN OUTMODED MODEL?

Given the state-centric history of anti-terrorism efforts, countering a non-territorial leaderless approach to international terrorism may require significant adaptation. Long before 9-11, a major thrust of the fight against terrorism focused on curtailing state sponsorship, a tactic that would be of less value in the absence of meaningful state patronage for terrorist organizations. The U.S. State Department's congressionally mandated list of state sponsors of terrorism may have helped draw lines between Washington's allies and enemies in the past, but the list will be of little use confronting those terrorists who refrain from centralized bases or leadership.

In the debates that took place in late 2002 and early 2003 about invading Iraq and toppling Saddam Hussein's regime, the Bush administration also relied on state-centric arguments for understanding contemporary terrorism. Senior Bush administration officials repeatedly argued that a war against Iraq constituted a central part of the post–September 11 war on terrorism. Whether the question was alleged ties between Al Qaeda and Iraq or Iraq's financial support for Palestinian suicide bombers, U.S. officials suggested that the absence of a state actor—Iraq—would weaken the terrorists.

The emphasis on ties between Al Qaeda and Iraq implied that the end of Saddam's regime would undermine the threat from Al Qaeda. On February 5, 2003, Secretary of State Colin Powell warned the UN Security Council that Iraq could help Al Qaeda to build more sophisticated bombs, forge documents, and acquire expertise on nonconventional weapons. On March 6, President Bush accused Iraq of providing "funding and training and safe haven to terrorists—terrorists who would willingly use weapons of mass destruction against America and other peace-loving countries." Even after the military campaign ended, Vice President Dick Cheney added that in "Iraq, we took another essential step in the war on terror." The same officials confidently asserted that a post-Saddam Iraq would greatly enhance global peace and security.

The Bush administration misunderstood or misrepresented the impact that regime change in Iraq would have on terrorist threats. Al Qaeda's recruitment, training, fundraising, and execution of attacks never depended on Iraq. As for Palestinian suicide bombers, they originate within the dynamic of the Israeli-Palestinian conflict, not as a response to external Iraqi financial incentives.

In assessing the Iraq debate, however, the point is not that the Bush administration framed the issue in terms of state sponsorship when it should have talked in terms of leaderless resistance. Al Qaeda and Palestinian bombers are not cases of leaderless resistance, either. As of late 2003, Osama bin Laden and others apparently continue to direct the organization. No overt territorial sanctuary has emerged to replace Afghanistan, but the mountainous areas in Afghanistan and Pakistan may be serving a similar purpose.

The Iraq debates instead demonstrate the continuing political and ideological appeal of state-centered arguments. Leaders probably framed the debate that way because it is how they have tended to look at the issue in the past. It is also how they assumed they could build public support for attacking Iraq. State-sponsorship of terrorist organizations is part of the entrenched conceptual model—and not without reason, given past experience. This way of thinking, however, may make it harder to fully grasp a shift to leaderless resistance if and when such a time arrives.

LEADERLESS AND LETHAL

The conceptual terrain is further complicated because the choice is not always between pure leaderless resistance and traditional state sponsorship. An organization could move from one model to the other over time or travel in the wide area of ambiguity in between. In this regard, the next generation of Islamist terrorists, whether Al Qaeda or other groups, will have an advantage over their predecessors.

Al Qaeda once had a base and a centralized leadership that did and still does articulate a justification for terrorist acts against the United States and its allies. Hundreds of millions, if not billions, of people around the world likely have heard or seen Al Qaeda videos and speeches. September 11 resulted in tremendous publicity for the cause, not to mention the joy bin Laden must have felt after being declared an enemy of the United States. Given all this attention to Al Qaeda, some individuals who currently are not Al Qaeda members may nonetheless be motivated to act violently. Moreover, thousands of fighters have already passed through Afghanistan. Even if the country no longer serves as a training camp, the wealth of existing experience may last for some years.

All this is not meant to suggest that leaderless resistance represents a superior or more threatening model for terrorist activities over traditional nation-based organizations. The most effective and deadly forms of terrorism, including actions carried out by terrorists who seek nonconventional weaponry, may still require a territorial sponsor or sanctuary. It does illustrate, however, that creating the conditions to deny terrorists territorial bases and leadership is not enough to bring an end to international terrorism.

Reprinted with permission from *Current History* magazine (December 2003). © 2007 Current History, Inc.

Terrorism could well be viewed as a modern version of an age-old exercise in violence. Its precise objectives might be shrouded in mystery, and it might function at times without a clear leadership hierarchy, but terrorism's deep roots in the history of extremism are there for all to see. In many ways, modern terror is merely a variation on tradition. It is undeniable, however, that something is different today. No one could be faulted for sensing a distinct change. It is a "new" terrorism that plagues the world, one that is unique in its scope, scale, and ferocity.

A core characteristic of this updated version of terrorism is a novel theatricality made possible by advances in global communications. Dramatic effect has always been a consideration in acts of extremist violence. This was true whether it meant assassinating a political figure in broad daylight or attacking a renowned public building or crowded meeting place. Television and the Internet, however, have vastly enlarged the stage upon which the aggression is acted out. Images of bloodshed and destruction circle the earth almost instantaneously, reaching into the homes and imaginations of billions of people. As the historian John A. Lynn has written, the "camera lens becomes a magnifying glass. And if terrorism is, as they say, grand theater, then the media fill the hall."[*] The bomb-throwing, dagger-wielding radicals of old could not have dreamed of the attention that modern terrorists receive.

Recognizing this new development in an ancient tradition, Mark Juergensmeyer labeled terrorism as "performance violence." Terrorism, in this case, becomes a dark form of street theater in which the audience plays a crucial role. Spectators witness and confirm the performances enacted by terrorist players. This corroboration is a vital prop in the larger "show" that terrorists put on. Driven by a belief that they are combating an evil cosmic foe, violent extremists must prove to the world the justice of their cause. For this, they require an audience. Terrorists, put simply, demand to be seen.

NOTES

[*] John A. Lynn, *Battle: A History of Combat and Culture* (Cambridge, Mass.: Westview Press, 2004), 326.

Understanding the New Terrorism
MARK JUERGENSMEYER

Any act of terrorism is disturbing, but what has come to be known as the "new terrorism" is especially disquieting. Its attacks appear random, its motives murky. Acts of violence that characterized the "old terrorism"—such as bombing police headquarters and assassinating political opponents—were often vicious. But they could be understood as tactics aimed at achieving clear-cut political goals. The new terrorism frightens by its unpredictability. The bombing of the World Trade Center in 1993 and, two years later, the unleashing of nerve gas in the Tokyo subway system and the shearing off of the entire front half of the Oklahoma City federal building in a truck-bomb explosion evoked widespread fear. These incidents, like the 1998 attack on American Embassies in Tanzania and Kenya, showed the vulnerability and fragility of the public order that we take for granted.

Of course, the old terrorism was also frightening. Like the newer version, it had been characterized by public acts of massive destruction aimed at creating widespread fear. The new terrorism, however, does this and more: it appears pointless since it does not lead directly to any strategic goal, and it seems exotic since it is frequently couched in the visionary rhetoric of religion. It is the anti-order of the new world order of the twenty-first century.

The new terrorism emerged in the 1980s from more traditional forms of political conflict in the Middle East. Gradually, along with pro-Palestinian acts of political violence, new strands of strident Muslim terrorism began to appear that were unrelated to the Palestinian or any other definable political cause. In Egypt President Anwar Sadat was assassinated by religious extremists and Hezbollah suicide bombers in Lebanon targeted symbols of American military power. By the mid-1990s religious-based terrorism aimed at the general population as well as at symbols of government power exploded throughout the world. Activists from virtually every religious tradition were involved: not only Islamic suicide bombers in the Middle East but also Christian militants in the United States, Jewish assassins in Israel, a terrorist Buddhist sect in Japan, and radical Sikhs and Hindus in India.

The last decade of the twentieth century was the decade of the new terrorism. In 1980 the United States State Department listing of international terrorist groups contained scarcely a single religious organization.

In 1998, when Secretary of State Madeleine Albright announced a list of 30 of the world's most dangerous groups, over half were religious and included Judaism, Islam, and Buddhism. If other violent religious groups around the world were added—including the many Christian militia and other paramilitary organizations found in the United States—the number of religious terrorist groups would be considerable. According to the 1995 RAND–St. Andrews Chronology of International Terrorist Incidents, the number of religious groups as a subset of all international terrorist organizations increased from 16 of 49 identified terrorist groups in 1994 to 26 of the 56 groups listed the following year.[1]

CULTURES OF VIOLENCE

What has prompted the new terrorism? Why have these acts often been associated with religious causes, and why are they occurring with such frequency at this moment in history? To answer these questions, I turned to the perpetrators themselves, those involved in terrorist acts or within the circles of supporters that comprise what I call "cultures of violence"—groups that view themselves as engaged in great struggles. While it was not my purpose to be sympathetic, I wanted to get to know them well enough to understand them and their worldviews. What puzzled me was not why bad things are done by bad people, but rather why bad things are often done by those who otherwise appear to be good—and in cases of the new terrorism, often pious people dedicated to moral visions of the world.

First I wanted to know why the violence of the new terrorism is so extreme. After all, these have been acts not only of destruction, but also of deliberately induced and vivid bloodshed. Each of these acts has seemed designed to magnify the savage nature of their violence, and meant to elicit anger. What is the point of such apparently pointless violence?

I posed this question to one of the men convicted of bombing the World Trade Center in 1995, Mahmud Abouhalima, who is alleged to have masterminded the conspiracy to destroy the buildings. We met on two occasions in the federal penitentiary in Lompoc, California—a maximum-security prison that prides itself as the new "rock," a formidable and secure successor to Alcatraz. Abouhalima was brought to an empty dining room to talk with me. When I first met him in August 1997, he was handcuffed and accompanied by three guards. Dressed in green prison garb, Abouhalima—tall, red-haired, his face freckled—spoke in English, his words fluid and colloquial. He leaned over as he spoke, often whispering, as if to reinforce the intimacy and importance of what he said.

Abouhalima was restricted in what he felt he could say, since he still hoped to appeal his case. He was, however, open about the subject that I wanted to discuss with him: the public role of Islam and its increasingly political impact. He also felt free to talk about terrorism generally and terrorist incidents of which he was not accused, such as the Oklahoma City federal building bombing.

In my second conversation with him a month later, Abouhalima discussed the case of one of the Oklahoma City defendants, Terry Nichols, who was being tried at the time. Abouhalima tried to help me understand the purposes of the Oklahoma bombing.

"It was done for a very, very specific reason," Abouhalima told me, contradicting any impression I might have had that the federal building was bombed for no reason at all. "They had some certain target, you know, a specific achievement," Abouhalima said. He added that "they wanted to reach the government with the message that we are not tolerating the way that you are dealing with our citizens." Although Abouhalima stopped short of comparing this incident with the bombing of the World Trade Center, I gathered that what he said about the Oklahoma City bombing could apply to similar events.

Was the bombing an act of terrorism? Abouhalima thought for a moment, then explained that the concept was "messed up." The term seemed to be used only for incidents of violence that people did not like, or rather, Abouhalima explained, for incidents the media have labeled terrorist.

"What about the United States government?" Abouhalima asked me. "How do they justify their acts of bombings, of killing innocent people, directly or indirectly, openly or secretly? They're killing people everywhere in the world: before, today, and tomorrow. How do you define that?" Then he described what he regarded as America's terrorist attitude toward the world. According to Abouhalima, the United States tries to "terrorize nations," to "obliterate their power," and to tell them that they "are nothing" and that they "have to follow us." Abouhalima implied that any form of international political or economic control was a form of terrorism. He also gave specific examples of where he felt the United States had used its power to kill indiscriminately.

"In Japan, for instance," Abouhalima said, referring to the atomic bomb blasts, "through the bombs, you know, that killed more than 200,000 people." Perhaps it was a coincidence, but that was also exactly the number of people officials estimated would have been killed in the

World Trade Center blast if the bomb had been placed differently and both towers were brought down, as allegedly had been planned.

Was the Oklahoma City blast a terrorist response to the government's terrorism? "That's what I'm saying," Abouhalima replied. "If they believe, if these guys, whoever they are, did whatever bombing they say they did in Oklahoma City, if they believe that the government unjustifiably killed the people in Waco, then they have their own way to respond.[2] They absolutely have their own way to respond."

"Yet," I said in an effort to put the Oklahoma City bombing in context, "it killed a lot of innocent people, and ultimately it did not seem to change anything."

"But it's as I said," Abouhalima responded, "at least the government got the message."

The message was this: the government was an enemy, a satanic foe. According to Abouhalima, the attack was meant to create a graphic and easily understandable object lesson. From Abouhalima's point of view, the Oklahoma City bombing succeeded because the world was made aware that a great struggle was under way.

PERFORMANCE VIOLENCE

I accepted Abouhalima's point that bombings like that carried out in Oklahoma City were powerful demonstrations of a worldview in which the United States government was evil. I also accepted his notion that such buildings were bombed for a reason—these were not the acts of madmen. But I hesitated to label these actions as part of a political strategy. Rather, they were dramatic events, intended to impress with their symbolic significance. As such, they could be analyzed as one would any other symbol, ritual, or sacred drama.

Imagine a line with "strategic" on the one side and "symbolic" on the other. Various acts of terrorism can be arrayed in between. The taking of hostages at the Japanese ambassador's residence by Túpac Amaru guerrillas in Peru in 1997—in part an attempt to leverage power to release members of the movement held prisoner by the Peruvian government—might be placed closer to the political, strategic side. The nerve gas attack on a Tokyo subway by the "new religion" Aum Shinrikyo in 1995 would be closer to the symbolic, religious side. Both were products of logical thought, and both had an internal rationale. Yet in the case of Aum's nerve gas attack, which was more symbolic than strategic, the logic was focused not on immediate political acquisitions, but on larger, less tangible goals.

The adjectives that we use to describe acts of the new terrorism—symbolic, dramatic, theatrical—suggest the idea of viewing them not as tactics but as performance violence. In using the term "performance" I knowingly invoke the idea of theater. This analogy is apt not only because terrorist acts are dramatic but also because they are conducted with an awareness of particular settings, appropriate timings, and the various audiences for the events. By discussing terrorism as performance I am not suggesting that such acts are undertaken lightly or capriciously. Rather, like religious ritual or street theater, they are dramas designed to have an impact on the several audiences they affect. Witnesses to the violence, even at a distance, through the news media, therefore are part of the incident itself.

The street theater of performance violence forces direct and indirect witnesses into the perpetrator's consciousness—into their alternative view of the world. This gives the perpetrators of terrorism a kind of celebrity status and their actions an illusion of importance. The novelist Don DeLillo, in *Mao II*, writes that the only person taken seriously in modern society is the "lethal believer, the person who kills and dies for faith." When we who observe the acts of such people take them seriously—when we are disgusted and repelled by them and begin to distrust the peacefulness of the world—the purposes of their theater have been achieved.

A CALL TO ARMS

If the new terrorism can be considered a form of street theater—as a kind of performance violence—acts of terrorism may be seen as an element in a dramatic script. These acts are imagined to be aspects of great conflicts—scenarios of ultimate significance that give meaning to violence and prescribe when, where, how, and for whom the actions are performed. In all the instances that I examined, these scenarios involved the idea of a great transcendent war.

Consider the case of the Reverend Michael Bray, a Lutheran pastor who served prison time for bombing abortion clinics in the eastern United States and who defended the actions of his friend, the Reverend Paul Hill, in killing an abortion clinic doctor and his bodyguard in Pensacola, Florida on July 29, 1994. Bray told me in an April 1996 interview that the world was at war. He said that it was necessary to kill and die over the issue of abortion, but not simply because abortion was immoral. Rather, Bray saw laws accepting abortion—and homosexuality, for that matter—as symptoms of a much greater issue.

From Bray's point of view, the world was embroiled in a war similar to World War II. "The issues are comparable," Bray told me, adding that the arguments that justified Christians in supporting violence at that time "now are the same." He pointed out that many German Christians felt guilty that they had failed to act with force against the Nazis when innocent Jews were being killed. Now, Bray reflected, Christians say to themselves, "would that we have moved earlier" to stop the killing. Bray compared this situation with the "killing" involved in abortion.

Bray was disturbed not only by the slaughter of what he described as the "unborn," but by what he felt was a Nazi-like attitude, a disregard for human life, and a penchant for indiscriminate killing that characterized the ruling powers of contemporary American society. This silent war deeply troubled him. He thought that overt rebellion or revolution against this power could occur only with an economic collapse or social chaos sufficiently catastrophic to make people aware of the situation, "to give people the strength or the zeal to take up arms." In the meantime, what he called "defensive acts" and what most Americans would call terrorism provided public reminders of the silent war, perhaps serving to alert Americans to join the rebellion.

Michael Bray's vision of a world caught in an imminent and almost eschatological confrontation between the forces of good and evil arrayed on the battlefield of politics is not idiosyncratic: it is remarkably similar to that of militant Sikhs in India, Aum Shinrikyo in Japan, Rabbi Meir Kahane's Kach party in Israel, Omar Abdul Rahman's circle of militant Muslims in Egypt and New Jersey. Theirs were acts of desperation in response to what they perceived as a world gone terribly awry. What was strikingly similar about the cultures of which they were a part was their view of the contemporary world at war.

In Japan, for example, the members of Aum Shinrikyo believed that the world was on the brink of a conflagration similar to World War II. What the Japanese remembered about that war was not so much the Nazi genocide as the annihilation of Japanese cities under the rain of American bombs, including the atomic bombs that destroyed Hiroshima and Nagasaki. According to Shoko Asahara, the spiritual master of Aum Shinrikyo, this reign of terror would soon return in a war that would be even more catastrophic than World War II. "The weapons used in World War III," Asahara told his followers, "will make the atomic and hydrogen bombs look like toys." Writing in 1995, Asahara predicted that the full force of the great war would not be apparent until 1999. But he tried to persuade his followers and the Japanese public that the first stages of Armageddon, as he called it, had already arrived at Japan's shores.

This Armageddon, Asahara said, would "completely annihilate the cities, produce a state of anarchy, and then establish a worldwide, unified political power." The shadowy forces behind this plot included Jewish capitalists, Freemasons, the United States Army, and the Japanese government. The takeover was so subtle, however, that most people were unaware of it.

The prophetic teachings of Aum Shinrikyo were deemed important because they allowed the enlightened few to be aware of the coming disaster and to prepare for it. As far as the group's members knew, the creation of nerve gas in Aum chemical laboratories was solely for the purpose of developing preventive medicines and devices. These would protect them against poisonous gasses once Armageddon arrived and chemical weapons were used against the populace. Only the most loyal were willing to believe these prophecies without any evidence that World War III was in fact beginning to occur. The release of nerve gas in the Tokyo subway provided dramatic proof that the war was at hand—or so Asahara's followers thought until it became clear that Asahara himself was implicated in the attack.

COSMIC WAR

Religious struggles in other parts of the world—even those that seem more rational because they are related to contests over the control of land for which both sides have a legitimate claim—nonetheless have employed images of warfare on a grand scale. Yochay Ron, a young Jewish activist with whom I spoke near Hebron, told me that the war with the Arabs did not begin with the intifada (uprising) in the 1980s, or even with the establishment of the state of Israel in 1948. It dated to "biblical times," Ron explained in an August 1995 interview, indicating that the present-day Arabs were simply the descendants of the ancient enemies of Israel described in the Bible against whom God unleashed wars of revenge. Ultimately Ron thought that the warfare would end, but only when Arabs left the land and Israel was, in his view, complete. Sarah Nachshon, who like Ron lived in the Beit Hadassah settlement in Hebron, also thought that the current violence was part of a spiritual conflict. "It's written in the Bible," she said, "that until the Messiah comes there will be a big war, and the war will be in Jerusalem."

The Palestinian conflict was conceived as being something larger than a contest between Arabs and Jews: it was a cosmic struggle of Manichaean proportions. This view was shared by religious activists on both sides. Sheik Ahmad Yasin, leader of the militant Islamic group

Hamas, for example, described the conflict in ultimate terms as the "combat between good and evil." A communiqué issued by Hamas after the United States sent troops to Saudi Arabia following Saddam Hussein's invasion of Kuwait in 1990, declared it to be "another episode in the fight between good and evil," and a "hateful Christian plot against our religion, our civilization, and our land." The absolutism of cosmic war has made compromise unlikely, and those who have suggested a negotiated settlement in the Israeli-Palestinian conflict have been excoriated as the enemy. The extremes on both sides prefer war over peace.

One reason why a state of war is preferable to peace is that it morally justifies violent acts. Violence, in turn, offers the illusion of power. Some Christian activists have claimed that in wartime the ends justify the means, thereby exonerating their attacks on a secular society they deem immoral. When asked if they would use poison to contaminate the water supply of a major American city, a member of the Phineas Priesthood, a sect of the Christian Identity white supremacist group that opposes interfaith marriages, said in October 1995, "when one is at war, one has to consider such things, unfortunately." Reverend Bray made an ethical distinction between what was legal in a peaceful society and what was morally justified in a situation of warfare: the latter included transgressing property rights and the laws against murder. Bray's argument was similar to that of the assassin of Mohandas Gandhi, Nathuram Godse, who in his court trial eloquently justified what he called his "moral" though "illegal" act of killing the Mahatma.

The idea of war is appealing because it justifies violence and imparts a peculiarly satisfying understanding of the world. Warfare implies more than an attitude. Ultimately it is a worldview and an assertion of power. To live in a state of war is to live in a world in which individuals know who they are, why they have suffered, by whose hand they have been humiliated, and at what expense they have persevered. It provides cosmology, history, and eschatology, and offers the reins of political control. Perhaps most important it holds out the hope of victory and the means to achieve it. In the images of cosmic war, this victorious triumph is a grand moment of social and personal transformation, transcending all worldly limitations. To live with these images of war is to live with hope itself.

RESPONDING TO THE NEW TERRORISM

How can we respond to such acts of terrorism—acts that are not only tactics in political strategies but performances of violence that symbolize a cosmic war? One temptation is to respond in kind, as the United States government did when Muslim activists—allegedly under the guidance of Osama bin Laden—bombed the American embassies in Kenya and Tanzania in 1998. But the acts of retaliation seemed to stray far from their marks. The cruise missiles launched by the United States military fell on a pharmaceutical plant in Sudan and a hillside in Afghanistan without achieving any obvious strategic objective. No significant damage was done to bin Laden's organization, nor did he or any other activist appear to be intimidated as a result of the missile attack.

A quid pro quo for terrorism usually fails, if for no other reason than few governments have been willing to sink to the same savage levels and adopt the same means of gutter combat that groups involved in terrorist acts have been willing to undertake. Moreover, governments have usually been aware that terrorists observe their responses to acts of terrorism. Any response, even in the form of retaliatory strikes, enhances the perpetrators' credibility.

Another, quite different response to terrorist acts is to do nothing violent in response. After the World Trade Center bombing, for instance, the United States government made no retaliatory raids on the perpetrators' bases of operations. In general this approach helps defuse a climate of violence. Government authorities are not goaded into military actions that fit into the war scenario the terrorists are trying to evoke. And without having provoked a response, activist groups might grow weary of their theory of cosmic war and abandon their random attacks. But then again, they might not.

A complete hands-off approach is also problematic: it might or might not quell violence. Moreover, terrorist acts are real threats to public safety, and no government can afford the perception by its citizens that it is too weak to respond when public order is under assault.

As a result, most governments adopt an appropriate middle road. They try to support and promote moderate leadership within communities of violence to diminish support for the extremists. They are also vigilant in their surveillance of potential terrorist groups to prevent the initial occurrence of violent acts. When terrorism does strike, the most prudent authorities attempt to apprehend the suspects legally without responding with the kind of force that will provoke more violence.

Governments also must act decisively to shore up their own legitimacy. Authorities must be swift to condemn perceived threats to public order. In the wake of a series of catastrophic terrorist assaults in the mid-1990s, for example, the American government felt compelled to speak out strongly against such actions. Secretary of State Warren Christopher assured the public that the United States government regarded terrorist acts in the name of religion and ethnic identity as "one of the most important security challenges we face in the wake of the Cold War."

Statements like Christopher's may be somewhat alarmist. The small bands of rogue activists who have blown up American embassies in Africa or unleashed nerve gas in Tokyo subways are not capable of mounting a major assault on the military might of the United States, and certainly do not have the ability to run their own organizations effectively, much less to seize the reins of power of major nation-states. In another sense, however, even small-scale acts of terrorism undertaken by a handful of angry activists constitute more than just a public nuisance. They create an aura of instability that threatens the credibility of nation-states.

TERRORISM AND GLOBAL CHANGE

Such assaults on public authority are unnerving because they come at a sensitive time. The last decade of the twentieth century and the first years of the twenty-first are a moment of transition on a global scale. With the fall of the Soviet Union and the end of the cold war in 1990 came the removal of a secure bipolar view of the world. In its wake appeared a rush of new expressions of local control. At the same time, local cultural identities are being threatened by new forces of globalization that have economic, technological, and cultural dimensions. People throughout the world are increasingly being linked to a vast global economic structure and subjected to images that invariably express the most superficial and secular aspects of popular culture in the West. New alliances are emerging in Asia, the Middle East, and Europe. As the twenty-first century dawns, it is not yet clear whether the new world order will consist of transnational entities, regional alliances, or nation-states—and if the latter, whether they will be modeled on the secular image of nations built on social contracts or on the religious ideal of states based on culture.

The public insecurity that has come with these global cataclysms has been felt not only in nations that have changed the most—countries in the former Soviet Union, for instance—but also in economically stronger societies. In the 1990s, for example, the United States saw a remarkable degree of disaffection with its political leaders and the rise of right-wing religious movements that fed on the public's perception of inherent government immorality.

Is the rise of religious terrorism related to these global changes? We know that some groups associated with violence in industrialized societies have had an antimodernist political agenda. At the extreme end of this religious rejection in the United States were members of the Christian militia and Christian Identity movement, and isolated groups such as the

Branch Davidian sect in Waco. When Michael Bray and other members of the religious right cast aspersions at the "new world order" they believe is being promoted by President Bill Clinton and the United Nations, what Bray and his colleagues fear is the imposition of an order both tyrannical and atheist. They see evidence of an antireligious governmental pogrom in a secular, multicultural society that has no religious moorings.

Acts of religious terrorism may be symptomatic of great global shifts in the structuring of public order. In such a climate, religion gives a profundity and ideological clarity to often real experiences of economic destitution, social oppression, political corruption, and a desperate need to rise above the limitations of modern life. The image of cosmic struggle has given these bitter experiences meaning, and the involvement in a grand conflict has been for some participants exhilarating and even empowering. Those engaged in this conflict have gained a sense of their own destinies. Acts of violence—even what appears to outsiders as vicious acts of terrorism—have been viewed by insiders in some cultures of violence as both appropriate and justified. It is one of the ironies of history that violence sometimes accompanies the images of the morality and hope that are offered by religion's renewed presence in public life.

NOTES

1. See Bruce Hoffman, *Inside Terrorism* (New York: Columbia University Press, 1998), p. 91.

2. The Oklahoma City bombing occurred on April 19, 1995, the same day two years earlier that federal agents had launched an assault on the compound of the Branch Davidians, an armed group of religious extremists in Waco, Texas. All the sect's members in the compound—more than 80 people, including 22 children—perished in a fire that broke out during the assault.

Reprinted with permission from *Current History* magazine (April 2000). © 2007 Current History, Inc.

Understanding the remodeled form and function of global terrorism certainly changes the way society views it, but this knowledge alone does little to provide a handy definition of the phenomenon. Calling terrorism "postmodern," "leaderless resistance," or "performance violence" is fine, but that does not provide the type of umbrella term that allows for routine discussion. Some sort of descriptive consensus must be reached, if for no other reason than building a common vocabulary that will let people search for a solution to the problem of extremism. The general phenomenon of terrorism, in other words, must be defined one way or another.

This pressing need for a shared set of givens has led scholars and governments alike to craft various definitions of terrorism. The FBI, for example, labels terrorism as "the unlawful use of force or violence against persons or property to intimidate or coerce a government, the civilian population, or any segment thereof, in furtherance of political or social objectives."* The Department of Defense calls terrorism the "calculated use of violence or the threat of violence to inculcate fear, intended to coerce governments or societies in pursuit of goals that are generally political, religious, or ideological."** These definitions, at first glance, appear to be complete, but each fails to distinguish between terrorism and other forms of irregular warfare, such as guerilla and insurgent operations, not to mention the fact that almost every legitimate war includes one or more of these terrorist uses of violence. Former British anti-terrorism agent Barry Davies, in fact, reminds his readers that terrorist attacks are so similar to other forms of violence that, "in the end, we must all arrive at our own definition of terrorism."***

Bruce Hoffman, in the following excerpt from his 1998 book *Inside Terrorism*, tries to pry terrorism away from its close relatives by recognizing its distinctions. Rather than attempting to say what terrorism is, Hoffman strives to state clearly what it is not. By reversing the normal pattern of definition, he may come as close as possible to offering up the elusive terrorist criteria that many people are seeking.

NOTES

* Clifford E. Simonsen and Jeremy R. Spindlove, eds., *Terrorism Today: The Past, The Players, The Future* (Upper Saddle River, N.J.: Prentice Hall, 2000), 19.
** Ibid.
*** Barry Davies, *Terrorism: Inside a World Phenomenon* (London: Virgin Books, 2003), 15.

Distinctions as a Path to Definition
BRUCE HOFFMAN

Guerrilla warfare is a good place to start. Terrorism is often confused or equated with, or treated as synonymous with, guerrilla warfare. This is not entirely surprising, since guerrillas often employ the same tactics (assassination, kidnapping, bombings of public gathering-places, hostage-taking, etc) for the same purposes (to intimidate or coerce, thereby affecting behaviour through the arousal of fear) as terrorists. In addition, both terrorists and guerrillas wear neither uniform nor identifying insignia and thus are often indistinguishable from noncombatants. However, despite the inclination to lump both terrorists and guerrillas into the same catch-all category of "irregulars," there are nonetheless fundamental differences between the two. "Guerrilla," for example, in its most widely accepted usage, is taken to refer to a numerically larger group of armed individuals,[82] who operate as a military unit, attack enemy military forces, and seize and hold territory (even if only ephemerally during daylight hours), while also exercising some form of sovereignty or control over a defined geographical area and its population. Terrorists, however, do not function in the open as armed units, generally do not attempt to seize or hold territory, deliberately avoid engaging enemy military forces in combat and rarely exercise any direct control or sovereignty either over territory or population.[83]

It is also useful to distinguish terrorists from ordinary criminals. Like terrorists, criminals use violence as a means to attaining a specific end. However, while the violent act itself may be similar—kidnapping, shooting, arson, for example—the purpose or motivation clearly is not. Whether the criminal employs violence as a means to obtain money, to acquire material goods, or to kill or injure a specific victim for pay, he is acting primarily for selfish, personal motivations (usually material gain). Moreover, unlike terrorism, the ordinary criminal's violent act is not designed or intended to have consequences or create psychological repercussions beyond the act itself. The criminal may of course use some short-term act of violence to "terrorize" his victim, such as waving a gun in the face of a bank clerk during a robbery in order to ensure the clerk's expeditious compliance. In these instances, however, the bank robber is conveying no "message" (political or otherwise) through his act of violence beyond facilitating the rapid handing over of his "loot." The criminal's act therefore is not meant to have any effect reaching beyond either the incident itself or the immediate victim. Further, the violence is neither conceived nor intended to convey any message to anyone other than the bank clerk himself, whose rapid cooperation is the robber's only objective. Perhaps most fundamentally, the criminal is not concerned with influencing or affecting public opinion: he simply wants to abscond with his money or accomplish his mercenary task in the quickest and easiest way possible so that he may reap his reward and enjoy the fruits of his labours. By contrast, the fundamental aim of the terrorist's violence is ultimately to change "the system"—about which the ordinary criminal, of course, couldn't care less.[84]

The terrorist is also very different from the lunatic assassin, who may use identical tactics (e.g. shooting, bombing) and perhaps even seeks the same objective (e.g. the death of a political figure). However, while the tactics and targets of terrorists and lone assassins are often identical, their purpose is not. Whereas the terrorist's goal is again ineluctably *political* (to change or fundamentally alter a political system through his violent act), the lunatic assassin's goal is more often intrinsically idiosyncratic, completely egocentric and deeply personal. John Hinckley, who tried to kill President Reagan in 1981 to impress the actress Jodie Foster, is a case in point. He acted not from political motivation or ideological conviction but to fulfill some profound personal quest (killing the president to impress his screen idol). Such entirely *apolitical* motivations can in no way be compared to the rationalizations used by the Narodnaya Volya to justify its campaign of tyrannicide against the tsar and his minions, nor even to the Irish Republican Army's efforts to assassinate Prime Minister Margaret Thatcher or her successor, John Major, in hopes of dramatically changing British policy towards Northern Ireland. Further, just as one person cannot credibly claim to be a political party, so a lone individual cannot be considered to constitute a terrorist group. In this respect, even though Sirhan Sirhan's assassination of presidential candidate and U.S. Senator Robert Kennedy in 1968 had a political motive (to protest against U.S. support for Israel), it is debatable whether the murder should be defined as a terrorist act since Sirhan belonged to no organized political group and acted entirely on his own, out of deep personal frustration and a profound animus that few others shared. To qualify as terrorism, violence must be perpetrated by some organizational entity with at least some conspiratorial structure and identifiable chain of command beyond a single individual acting on his or her own.

Finally, the point should be emphasized that, unlike the ordinary criminal or the lunatic assassin, the terrorist is not pursuing purely egocentric goals—he is not driven by the wish to line his own pocket or satisfy some personal need or grievance. The terrorist is fundamentally an *altruist:* he believes that he is serving a "good" cause designed to achieve a greater good for a wider constituency—whether real or imagined—which the terrorist and his organization purport to represent. The criminal, by comparison, serves no cause at all, just his own personal aggrandizement and material satiation. Indeed, a "terrorist without a cause (at least in his own mind)," Konrad Kellen has argued, "is not a terrorist."[85] Yet the possession or identification of a cause is not a sufficient criterion for labelling someone a terrorist. In this key respect, the difference between terrorists and political extremists is clear. Many persons, of course, harbour all sorts of radical and extreme beliefs and opinions, and many of them belong to radical or even illegal or proscribed political organizations. However, if they do not use violence in the pursuance of their beliefs, they cannot be considered terrorists. The terrorist is fundamentally a *violent intellectual,* prepared to use and indeed committed to using force in the attainment of his goals.

By distinguishing terrorists from other types of criminals and terrorism from other forms of crime, we come to appreciate that terrorism is

- ineluctably political in aims and motives;
- violent—or, equally important, threatens violence;
- designed to have far-reaching psychological repercussions beyond the immediate victim or target;
- conducted by an organization with an identifiable chain of command or conspiratorial cell structure (whose members wear no uniform or identifying insignia); and
- perpetrated by a subnational group or non-state entity.

We may therefore now attempt to define terrorism as the deliberate creation and exploitation of fear through violence or the threat of violence in the pursuit of political change. All terrorist acts involve violence or the threat of violence. Terrorism is specifically designed to have far-reaching psychological effects beyond the immediate victim(s) or object of the terrorist attack. It is meant to instill fear within, and thereby intimidate, a wider "target audience" that might include a rival ethnic or religious group, an entire country, a national government or political party, or public opinion in general. Terrorism is designed to create power where there is none or to consolidate power where there is very little. Through the publicity generated by their violence, terrorists seek to obtain the leverage, influence and power they otherwise lack to effect political change on either a local or an international scale.

NOTES

82. International Institute for Strategic Studies, *Strategic Survey 2003/4*, p. 8. In its *Staff Report No. 16*, the National Commission on Terrorist Attacks Upon the United States ("9/11 Commission") notes on p. 16 that the 9/11 operation cost between $400,000 and $500,000 to mount.

83. Anonymous, *Imperial Hubris: Why the West is Losing the War on Terror* (Washington, D.C.: Brassey's. 2004), pp. 138-39.

84. See U.S. District Court, Southern District of New York, 1734HA01, *United States of America v. Mokhtar Haouri*, S4 00 Cr. 15 (JFK), June 3, 2001, pp. 538, 548, 589, 622, 658, 697.

85. See General Intelligence and Security Service, *Recruitment for the Jihad in the Netherlands: From Incident to Trend* (The Hague: Ministry of the Interior and Kingdom Relations, December 2002).

From *Inside Terrorism*, by Bruce Hoffman. Copyright © 1998 Columbia University Press. Reprinted with permission of the publisher.

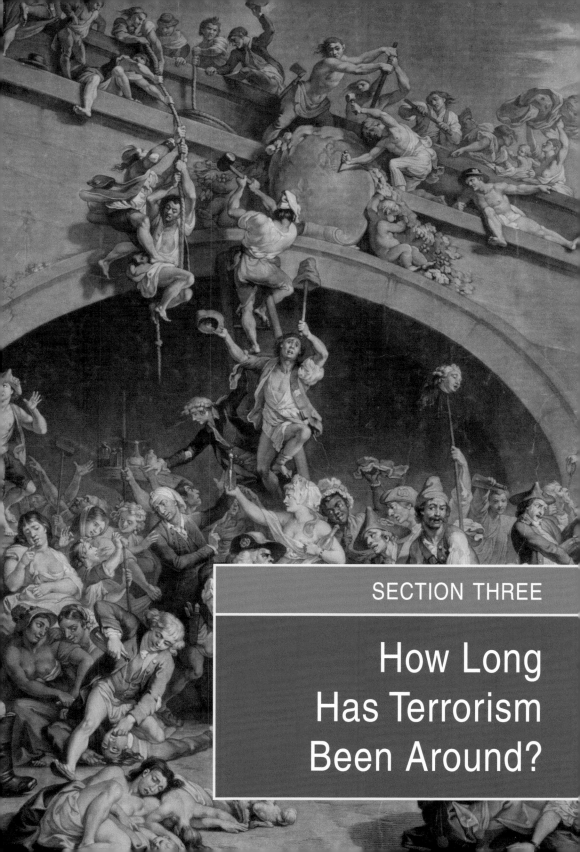

How Long
Has Terrorism
Been Around?

Like every other human artifact, terrorism has a history. Terrorism is embedded within a past filled with episodes of violence aimed at causing some sort of political or social change. Writer Caleb Carr is one of many commentators who recognize the violent heritage of which terrorism is a part. Carr, placing terrorism firmly into context, identifies it as merely "the current stage in a violent evolution whose origins extend as far back as does human conflict itself."* He goes on to argue that terrorism is fundamentally "a form of warfare," similar in many ways to so many others that preceded it.**

People could argue about terrorism's specific connections to older types of mass violence, but one thing is certain—this kind of aggression is assuredly not new. To be sure, as other authors in this volume have demonstrated, terrorist operations today differ markedly from those of even 50 or 60 years ago. Still, the extremism that the world sees today could well be thought of as just the latest variation on an ancient theme. Knives, firearms, explosives, and myriad other weapons have been employed, at one time or another, in the pursuit of change through destruction. Working alone or in groups, men and women have sought to alter various social and governmental systems through fear, intimidation, and murder.

Walter Laqueur makes this point in the following survey of terrorism's history, taken from his 1999 book *The New Terrorism*. Laqueur acknowledges modern terrorism's novel aspect, but nonetheless places it on a continuum of violence that stretches back across the centuries. During this time, the methods, means, and goals of violent extremists have evolved, with many becoming extinct. Yet the essential impulse, the urge by a minority to use force in an effort to alter the lives of the majority, has remained alive.

NOTES

*   Caleb Carr, *The Lessons of Terror: A History of Warfare Against Civilians* (New York: Random House, 2003), 6.
**   Ibid., 12.

Terrorism and History
WALTER LAQUEUR

Terrorism is violence, but not every form of violence is terrorism. It is vitally important to recognize that terrorism, although difficult to define precisely, as this brief history will show, is not a synonym for civil war, banditry, or guerrilla warfare.

The term *guerrilla* often has a positive connotation in our language, whereas *terrorism* almost always has a negative meaning. British and French news media will take a dim view of those engaging in terrorist operations in London and Paris, and will not hesitate to call the perpetrators "terrorists." But they are more reluctant to use such harsh terms with regard to those throwing bombs in distant countries, preferring more neutral terms such as "gunmen," "Militants," Islamic or otherwise, or indeed "urban guerrilla." In fact, the term *urban guerrilla* is a contradiction in terms. The strategy of guerrilla warfare is to liberate territory, to establish counterinstitutions and eventually a regular army, and this is possible in jungles, mountains, or other sparsely inhabited zones. The classic case of guerrilla warfare is China in the 1930s and 1940s; others, such as Vietnam's defeat of the French colonials and Castro's struggle in Cuba, are roughly similar. It is virtually impossible to establish free zones in a city, and for this reason the inaccurate and misleading term *urban guerrilla* is usually politically motivated or based on simple misunderstanding of the difference between the guerrilla and the terrorist. What makes the situation even more complicated is the fact that quite often guerrillas engage in terrorist acts both in the countryside and in urban centers. Algeria in the 1990s is a dramatic example.

There are other misunderstandings concerning the motives and the character of terrorism. For a long time there has been resistance in some circles to the use of the term to apply to small groups of people who engage in futile violence against the political establishment or certain sections of society. It was argued that the term should be reserved for states. It is perfectly true that tyrannies have caused infinitely more harm in history than terrorists, but it is hardly a relevant argument; with equal justice one could claim that it is not worthwhile to look for a cure for AIDS because this disease kills fewer people than cancer or heart disease, or that teaching French should be discontinued because there are twenty times as many Chinese as French people in the world.

During the 1960s and 1970s, when most terrorism was vaguely left wing in inspiration, arguments were made that terrorism was a response to injustice. Hence, if there were more political, social, and economic justice, terrorism would more or less automatically vanish. Seen in this light, terrorists were fanatical believers in justice driven to despair by intolerable conditions. But in the 1980s and '90s, when most terrorism in Europe and America came from the extreme right and the victims were foreigners, national minorities, or arbitrarily chosen, those who had previously shown understanding or even approval of terrorism no longer used these arguments. They could not longer possibly explain, let alone justify, murder with reference to political, social, or economic justice.

At the other extreme, it has been proclaimed that all and every form of terrorism is morally wrong. But such a total condemnation of violence is hardly tenable in the light of history. Catholic theologians in the Middle Ages found arguments in favor of killing tyrants, and more recently, the attempted assassination of Hitler and the successful killing of Heydrich, Hitler's man in Prague, among many other examples, can hardly be considered morally reprehensible. Terrorism might be the only feasible means of overthrowing a cruel dictatorship, the last resort of free men and women facing intolerable persecution. In such conditions, terrorism could be a moral imperative rather than a crime—the killing of a Hitler or a Stalin earlier on in his career would have saved the lives of millions of people.

The trouble with terrorism is not that is has always been indefensible but that it has been chosen more often than not as the prima ratio of self-appointed saviors of freedom and justice, of fanatics and madmen, not as the ultimate ratio of rebels against real tyranny.

ZEALOTS AND ASSASSINS

Political murder appears in the earliest annals of mankind, including the Bible. The stories of Judith and Holofernes, of Jael and Sisara the Old Testament heroes and villains, have provided inspiration to painters as well as to theologians and moral philosophers for ages. Seneca wrote that no sacrifice was as pleasing to the gods as the blood of a tyrant, and Cicero notes that tyrants always attracted a violent end. Harmodius and Aristogeiton, who killed the tyrant Hipparchus, were executed, but a statue was erected in their honor soon after. The civic virtues of Brutus were praised by his fellow Romans, but history—and Shakespeare—were of two minds about whether the murderer of Caesar was an honorable man.

The murder of oppressive rulers continued throughout history. It played an important role in the history of the Roman Empire. The emperors Caligula and Domitian were assassinated, as were Comodius and Elagabal, sometimes by their families, sometimes by their praetorian guards, and sometimes by their enemies (probably a few others were poisoned). Similar events can be found in the history of Byzantium.

The assassination of individuals has its origins in the prehistory of modern terrorism, but it is of course not quite the same. Historical terrorism almost always involves more than a single assassin and the carrying out of more than one operation. An exception may be the assassination of King Henri IV by a fanatic who believed that he had carried out a mission imposed on him by God; it might have been part of a conspiracy, but this we shall never know, because his interrogators were not very eager to find out. Another famous example from the same century was certainly part of an intrigue: the murder of Wallenstein, the famous seventeenth-century warlord. Historically, the favorite murder weapon has been the dagger, even through there were a few exceptions; William the Silent, Prince of Orange, was shot in Holland in 1584, when rifles and pistols were still new devices.

ORIGINS OF TERRORISM

There were also organized group committed to systematic terrorism early in recorded human history. From Josephus Flavius's writings, a great deal is known about the *sicari*, an extreme Jewish faction, who were active after the Roman occupation of Palestine (they gave us the word "zealot"). They were also involved in the siege of and the collective suicide at Masada. These patriots (or ultrapatriots, as they would be called in a later age) attacked their enemies, mainly other Jews, by daylight, very often during the celebrations of holidays, using a short dagger (*sica*) hidden under their coats. It was reported that they killed one high priest, burned the house of another, and torched the archives and the palace of the Herodian dynasts. There seems to have been asocial element as well: their attacks were also directed against moneylenders. Whereas the zealots engaged in guerrilla warfare against the Romans outside the cities, they apparently concentrated their terrorist activities in Jerusalem. When the revolt of the year 66 took place, the *sicari* were actively involved; one of them was the commander of the fortress Masada. Josephus called them brigands of a new type, and he considered them mainly responsible for the national catastrophe of the year 70, when the second Temple was destroyed and the Jewish state ceased to exist.

Another early example of terrorists is the Order of the Assassins in the eleventh century, an offshoot of the Ismailis, a Muslim sect. Hassan I Sabah, the founder of the order, was born in Qom, the Shiite center in northern Persia. Sabah adopted an extreme form of Ismaili doctrine that called for the seizure of several mountain fortresses; the first such fortress, Alamut, was seized in 1090. Years later the Assassins decided to transfer their activities from remote mountain regions to the main urban centers. Their first urban victim was the chief minister of the Sultan of Baghdad, Nazim al Mulq, a Sunnite by religious persuasion and there-fore an enemy. During the years that followed, Assassins were active in Persia, Syria, and Palestine, killing a great number of enemies, mainly Sunnites but also Christians, including Count Raymond II of Tripoli in Syria and Marquis Conrad of Montferrat, who ruled the kingdom of Jerusalem. There was a great deal of mystery about this movement and its master, owing to both the secrecy of its actions and the dissimulation used. Montferrat, for instance, was killed by a small group of emissaries who had disguised themselves as monks.

Seen in retrospect, the impact of the Assassins was small—they did not make many converts outside their mountain fortress, nor did they produce any significant changes in Muslim thought or practice. Alamut was occupied by Mongol invaders around 1270, but the Assassins had ceased to be a major force well before then. (Their main contribution was perhaps originating the strategy of the terrorist disguised—*taqfir*, or deception—as a devout emissary but in fact on a suicide mission, in exchange for which he was guaranteed the joys of paradise.)

Despite the considerable violence in Europe during the Middle Ages and, even worse, during the religious wars of the sixteenth and sev-enteenth centuries, in which monarchs as well as religious leaders were killed, there were no sustained terrorist campaigns during this time.

In cultures such as China and India secret societies have flourished from time immemorial. Many of these societies practiced violence and had their "enforcers." Their motivation was usually religious more than political, even though there was a pronounced element of xenophobia in both cases, such as the attacks against "foreign devils" culminating in the Boxer Rebellion of 1900. In India, the motivation of the *thuggee* (from which we get the word "thug"), who strangled their victims, was appar-ently to make an act of sacrifice to the goddess Kali.

The Chinese gangs of three or four hundred years ago had their own subculture, which practiced alternative medicine and meditation coupled with belief in all kinds of magic formulas. But they were not ascetic mil-lenarians, as the Assassins are believed to have been, and they had more in common with the Mafia than with modern political terrorism.

MODERN TERRORISM

The nineteenth century, a time of great national tension and social ferment, witnessed the emergence of both modern—what I will call "traditional"—terrorism and guerrilla warfare. Guerrilla warfare appeared first in the framework of the Napoleonic Wars in Spain and Russia, then continued in various parts of Asia and Africa, and reached its high tide after the Second World War with the disintegration of the European empires. Terrorism as we know it grew out of the secret societies of Italian and Irish patriots, but it also manifested itself in most Balkan countries, in Turkey and Egypt, and of course among the extreme Anarchists, who believed in the strategy of propaganda by deed. Last but not least were the Russian terrorists, who prior to the First World War were by far the most active and successful. Terrorism was widely discussed among the European far left, not because the use of violence as a political statement was a monopoly of the left but because the right was the political establishment, and prior to World War I the left was the agent of change, trying to overthrow the party in power. However, most leaders of the left rejected terrorism for both philosophical and practical reasons. They favored collective action, such as strikes, demonstrations, perhaps even insurgency, but neither Marx nor the anti-Marxists of the left believed in the "philosophy of the bomb." They gave political support to the Irish patriots and the Russian revolutionaries without necessarily embracing their tactics.

THE PHILOSOPHERS OF MASS DESTRUCTION

The two main exceptions to this aversion to terrorism were Karl Heinzen and Johann Most, German radicals who pioneered the philosophy of using weapons of mass destruction and a more or less systematic doctrine of terrorism. Both believed that murder was a political necessity. Both left their native country and migrated to the United State, and both were theoreticians of terrorism—but, ironically, not practitioners of the activities they recommended in their writings.

Heinzen, a radical democrat, blamed the revolutionaries of 1848 for not having shown enough resolution and ruthlessness. The key to revolution, as he saw it, was in improved technology. He anticipated weapons of mass destruction such as rockets, poison gases, and land mines, that one day would destroy whole cities with 100,000 inhabitants, and he advocated prizes for research in fields such as the poisoning of food. Heinzen was firmly convinced that the cause of freedom, in which he fervently believed, would not prevail without the use of poison and explosives. But neither in Louisville, Kentucky, nor in Boston, where he later lived and is now buried, did he practice what he preached. The Sage of Roxbury (as he was called in radical circles in his later years) became a staunch fighter for women's rights and one of the extreme spokesmen of abolitionism; he was a collaborator of William Lloyd Garrison, Horace Greeley, and Wendell Philips and a supporter of Abraham Lincoln. He attacked Marx, perhaps prophetically, since he believed communism would lead only to a new form of slavery. In a communist America, he wrote, he would not be permitted to travel from Boston to New York, to make a speech in favor of communism, without having official permission to do so. On his grave, in a cemetery in the Boston suburb of Forest Hill, there are two inscriptions, one in German to the effect that "Freedom inspired my spirit, truth rejuvenated my heart," and one in English: "His life work—the elevation of mankind."

Johann Most belongs to a younger generation. Having been a radical social democrat in his native country, he came to America in the early 1880s. His New York–based newspaper, *Freiheit*, became the most influential Anarchist organ in the world. Most did not believe in patient organizational and propagandistic work; people were always ready for a revolution, he believed, and all that was needed was a small minority to show the lead. The present system was essentially barbaric and could be destroyed only by barbaric means.

For the masses to be free, as Most saw it, the rulers had to be killed. Dynamite and poison, fire and the sword, were much more telling than a thousand revolutionary speeches. Most did not rule out propaganda in principle, but it had to be propaganda by deed, sowing confusion among the rulers and mobilizing the masses.

Most fully appreciated the importance of the media, which he knew could publicize a terrorist action all over the globe. He pioneered the concept of the letter bomb, even though the technical difficulties in producing such bombs were still enormous at the time, and, although then a flight of fancy, he imagined aerial terrorist attacks. He predicted that it would be possible to throw bombs from the air on military parades attended by emperors and tsars. Like Heinzen, Most believed that science would give terrorists a great advantage over their enemies through the invention of new weapons. He was also one of the first to advocate indiscriminate bombing; the terrorist could not afford to be guided by considerations of chivalry against an oppressive and powerful enemy. Bombs had to be put wherever the enemy, defined as "the upper ten thousand," meaning the aristocracy and the very rich, congregated, be it a church or a dance hall.

In later years, beginning about 1890, Most mellowed inasmuch as he favored a dual strategy, putting somewhat greater emphasis on political action and propaganda. Killing enemy leaders was important, but obtaining large sums of money was even more essential; he who could somehow obtain $100 million to he used for agitation and propaganda could do mankind a greater service by doing so than by killing ten monarchs. Terrorist acts per se meant little unless they were carried out at the right time and the right place. He accepted that there had to be a division of labor between a political movement and its terrorist arm. Not every political revolutionary was him to be a terrorist; in fact, the less political leaders knew about terrorism, the better for everyone concerned.

In his younger years Most had worked for a while in an ammunition factory in Jersey City, and, based partly on his own experience with dynamite and partly on a book published by the Austrian General Staff, he wrote a little book on revolutionary warfare. This book became the inspiration for *The Anarchist Cookbook*, a book that was published by a faction of the American New Left in the 1960s and that remains a standard text in terrorist circles. (There have been similar texts issued by extremists in recent years, but all of them owe a debt of gratitude to Most.)

The New York atmosphere where Most lived in later years softened him. Gradually, his German group with its beer evenings, weekend excursions, and amateur theatricals came to resemble more a club, a Verein, than a terrorist action group. Most was not a practicing terrorist, and though he was a leading figure on the extreme left in the United States, the police did not regard him as a very dangerous man. They by and large left him alone and did not even ban his periodical and books.

The third great nineteenth-century theoretician of terrorism, and the best known by far, was Michael Bakunin. He was active in Russia as well as in Germany (during the revolution of 1848), and in France and Switzerland. In his *Principles of Revolution,* published in 1869, Bakunin wrote that he and his friends recognized no other action except destruction—through poison, knife, rope, etc. Their final aim was revolution: evil could he eradicated only by violence; Russian soil could he cleansed only by sword and fire.

Bakunin also published the *Revolutionary Catechism,* which presented the rules of conduct for terrorists. The terrorist, according to Bakunin, was a lost soul, without interests, belongings, or ties of family or friendship; he was nameless. (The idea of the anonymous terrorist was later taken up by other terrorist movements whose members were known by number rather than by name.) The terrorist had broken with society and its laws and conventions, and he was consumed by one passion: the revolution.

Hard on himself, he had to he hard on others. Bakunin also provided tactical advice about infiltrating the old order by way of disguise and dissimulation, the Islamic *taqfir* in Russian style. The army, the bureaucracy, the world of business, and especially the church and the royal palace were all targets of infiltration.

He recommended that terrorists single out the most capable and intelligent enemies and kill them first, for such assassinations would inspire fear among society and the government. They should pretend to be friendly toward liberals and other well-wishers, even though these were dubious elements, only a few of whom would eventually become useful revolutionaries. A closing reference is made in this catechism to robbers and brigands, the only truly revolutionary element in society; if they would only unite and make common cause with the terrorists, they would he come a terrible and invincible power. Seen in historical perspective Bakunin was, among many other things, also the ideological precursor of a tactical alliance between terrorists and crime syndicates, though it is doubtful he would have thought so highly of the revolutionary potential of the Mafia or the Cali drug syndicate.

The catechism stresses time and again the need for total destruction. Institutions, social structures, civilization, and morality are to be destroyed root and branch. Yet, in the last resort, Bakunin, like Heinzen and Most, lacked the stamina and the ruthlessness to carry out his own program. This was left to small groups of Russian terrorists. The duo of Nechaev and Ishutin are an example, but the groups they purported to lead, with grandiloquent names such as "European Revolutionary Committee," were largely a figment of their imagination. Although they would occasionally kill one of their own members whom they suspected of treason, they did not cause physical harm to anyone else. Ishutin's largely imaginary terrorist group, called "Hell," was an interesting anticipation of the millennial sects of the next century.

Ironically, when the Russian terrorist movement of the late 1870s emerged, and culminated in the assassination of the tsar, its characteristics were very different from those described by Bakunin. Bakunin is remembered today mainly as one of the godfathers of modern anarchism, as a critic of Marx and Engels, and not as a terrorist.

WORDS INTO DEEDS

The two important terrorist exploits of the nineteenth century occurred in March 1881 and May 1882, respectively: the murder of Tsar Alexander II, and the assassination of Lord Cavendish and Thomas

Henry Burke, the chief secretary of the British administration in Ireland and one of his principal aides. Neither event came out of the blue. As in Ireland, there had been a revolutionary tradition in Russia antedating the murder of the tsar by many years, but it was not necessarily terrorist in character. Even the Narodnaya Volya (People's Will), which was eventually to carry out the assassination of the tsar, began its political activities trying to propagate the idea of an uprising among the peasants, a venture that, not surprisingly, ended in total failure since the revolutionaries' aims were not those of the villagers. A split ensued among the revolutionaries, with the terrorists claiming that killing leading opponents was far more cost effective than the Marxists' preference for political action. A small number of people could cause a great deal of havoc if ten or fifteen pillars of the establishment were murdered at once; the government would panic and the masses would wake up. But the Russian ideologists of terrorism never made it quite clear whether they expected the government simply to collapse and disintegrate, or whether a popular uprising would have to take place. The early terrorists were convinced that this stage could be reached within two or three years. If, on the other hand, the government was ready to make far-reaching concessions, such as granting freedom of speech and the right to organize, the terrorists might cease their campaign and reconsider the situation.

The tsar's assassination was prefaced in the year 1878 by the first major terrorist operation, the shooting of General Trepov, the governor of Moscow, by Vera Figner. The mood of public opinion was such that Figner was acquitted in the ensuing trial. True, at the time the majority of her comrades still thought that if there had to he armed struggle, it was to be "class against class," for the enemy was capitalism rather than the state, and they thought that the state might remain neutral in this battle. In the meantime, Nikolai Mezentsev, the head of the political police, had also been shot because of his role in the arrest and mistreatment of members of the People's Will group, and soon the organization was debating the fate of Mezentsev's successor, Drenteln. By that time the majority of the group had been won over to terrorism and the belief that a terrorist strategy would lead to quick successes. The revolutionary tribunals would pass their sentences; the militants would carry them out and then disappear without a trace.

The political views of the militants were at times very extreme, at others quite moderate, but they seemed not to have been very deeply held. Two of the most active terrorists, Tikhomirov and Romanenko, moved in later years to the extreme right, while another, Morozov, became a follower of the centrist Kadets. The terrorists proclaimed that they were fighting not only against naked tyranny, as in Russia, hut also constitutional repression, as in Germany; they would not hesitate to assassinate a dictator like Bismarck, even though he was governing in a semidemocratic framework. On the other hand, two weeks after the assassination of Emperor Alexander II, the executive committee of Narodnaya Volya stated in an open letter to his successor that terrorism was an unfortunate necessity, and that all they wanted was a general amnesty and a constitution granting elementary freedoms. It was said in later years, not without justification, that the terrorists were not really extremists but "liberals with a bomb," that in the prevailing state of repression even mild and moderate people would join the terrorists because their conscience dictated such a course of action.

Seen in this light, terrorism was merely a manifestation of the general crisis in Russian society. Vera Figner, whose attack had started it all, wrote in later years that terror had been like a major storm in an enclosed space: "The waves were rising high but the unrest did not spread. It exhausted the moral force of the intelligentsia." After the murder of the tsar, most of the assailants were quickly apprehended and executed, and there was relative quiet on the Russian home front for twenty years. The number of conspirators had been small, and while they enjoyed considerable sympathies among the intelligentsia and the middle class in general, there were not enough replacements to continue the struggle. They were all very young and many of them were students, but there were also some young women and workers among them, the latter including Zhelyabov, who headed the operation against the tsar.

Seen in historical perspective, the terrorism of Narodnaya Volya was counterproductive. The reformer Tsar Alexander II was replaced by the more repressive regime of Alexander III. The assassination helped to shut the door to a political solution of the constant Russian crisis and led to the revolution in 1917. The tsarist regime bore principal responsibility for the events of 1917, but the activities of the terrorists, despite their political aims, had not helped to resolve the continuing political crisis.

The tradition of Narodnaya Volya, or People's Will, lingered on, but a second wave of organized, systematic terrorism began with the foundation of the Social Revolutionary Party in 1900. Unlike its predecessor, this party practiced political action in combination with industrial strikes and agrarian uprisings, and, in contrast to the Marxist Social Democrats, they supported terrorism. It established an armed wing, the BO (Boevaya Organisatsia—Fighting Organization), whose exploits shook the government to its foundations. There was greater support in society for terrorism than there had been twenty-five years earlier, and after the murder of Plehwe, the hated minister of the interior, even some leading Social Democrats considered supporting terrorism in certain circumstances. Among the more prominent victims of terror were the minister of education; two ministers of the interior; two police chiefs of Moscow; Stolypin, the prime minister; and Grand Duke Serge Aleksandrovich, governor general of Moscow,

An important difference between the second and the first wave of terrorism was the sheer magnitude of the terrorist campaign. Whereas the People's Will operations had been concentrated almost entirely in the two major cities, Social Revolutionary terrorism was active throughout the country. The governor generals of Finland and the Caucasus were killed, and there were many assassinations in other border areas, including Armenia and Poland, and in minor cities.

Following the general lawlessness and temporary loss of power of the government during the Russo-Japanese War (1904–5), kidnappings, bank robberies, and other "expropriations" took place. No leader in the established system felt himself secure, and a mood of defeatism spread through the country. The revolution of 1905 brought about certain concessions on the part of the government in the form of a constitution. This, in turn, caused a decline in terrorist activity, for if political action, strikes, and demonstrations could bring about results, it seemed pointless to engage in terrorism. But the tsarist regime recovered much of the lost ground as the revolutionary impetus ran out of steam, and while terrorist activities were resumed in 1906, including some spectacular acts of violence, the authorities succeeded in imposing their will.

The BO was successfully penetrated by police agents; the head of the organization, Azev, and many others turned out to be police spies. Azev's comrades refused to believe in his deception for a long time, but once this had been proven, the fighting spirit of the militants rapidly disintegrated in a general climate of mutual distrust. It is also true that whereas earlier the tsarist government had observed legal niceties, after 1906 it introduced a state of siege in many parts of Russia. Those apprehended were dealt with by court martial, and draconian measures were used without compunction. The number of death sentences rose from 144 in 1906 to 1,139 in 1907, and 825 were handed down in 1908. The total number of executions was in the thousands, and an even greater number of people were sentenced to hard labor. Taking into account that not all terrorists were apprehended, it is clear that the sheer scale of terrorism in Russia was unprecedented. And yet terrorism did not succeed in overthrowing the regime. The murder of Stolypin the prime minister in 1911 caused no political reverberations, and there were no major terrorist attacks during the years leading up to the revolution of 1917.

TERRORISM IN THE TWENTIETH CENTURY

Toward the end of the nineteenth century and up to the outbreak of the First World War, terrorist attacks took place in many places all over the globe. They were widespread in the Ottoman Empire, then in its last phase of disintegration. Armenian terrorism against the Turks began in the 1890s but ended in disaster with the mass murder of Armenians in World War I. This terrorist tradition among the Armenians continued outside Turkey after the massacres of the First World War and was directed against individual Turkish military leaders. There was a third wave of Armenian terrorism in the late 1970s and 1980s, when the Turkish ambassadors to Austria and France were killed.

Another terrorist group was IMRO, the Macedonian Revolutionary Organization, which for almost three decades engaged not only in terrorism but in political activity and in the preparation for a mass insurrection. The longevity of sustained Macedonian terrorism can be explained with reference to the support it received (in contrast to the Armenians) from governments protecting them, mainly the Bulgarians. The price the IMRO had to pay was high, because it became for all intents and purposes a tool of the Bulgarian government, and was used mainly against Yugoslavia as well as against domestic enemies. IMRO dependence on Sofia led eventually to internal splits and internecine warfare—more Macedonians were killed by IMRO than were enemies of Macedonian statehood. In the end Macedonia did not gain independence, except in part—and only very recently—after the disintegration of Yugoslavia.

Terrorism also occurred in India and Japan. Two prime ministers were killed in Tokyo toward the end of the last century, another in 1932, not to mention a variety of other government ministers. There was even an attempted assassination of the emperor. In India political murders became frequent during the decade prior to World War I, but a Viceroy, Lord Mayo, had been killed as far back as 1872.

The most striking terrorist movement prior to World War I was that of the anarchists, whose deeds all over Europe preoccupied public opinion, police chiefs, psychologists, and writers, including Henry James and Joseph Conrad, for many years. The French anarchists Ravachol, Auguste Vaillant, and Emile Henri created an enormous stir, giving the impression of a giant conspiracy, which, in fact, never existed. Ravachol was a bandit who would have robbed and killed even if anarchism had never existed;

Vaiflant was a bohemian; and Emile Henri was an excited and excitable young man. The three really did not have much in common. But as far as the general public was concerned, anarchists, socialists, and radicals were all birds of a feather. Governments and police chiefs probably knew better, although they saw no reason to correct this mistaken impression.

The panic was not entirely unjustified, inasmuch as there were a great many attempts on the life of leading statesmen between the 1880s and the first decade of the twentieth century. American presidents Garfield and McKinley were among those killed. There were several attempts to assassinate Bismarck and Emperor Wilhelm I of Germany. French president Carnot was killed in 1894; Antonio Canovas, the Spanish prime minister, in 1897; Empress Elizabeth (Zita) of Austria in 1898; and King Umberto of Italy in 1900. If one adds the sizable number of lesser figures and, of course, the Russian rulers and politicians, it should come as no surprise that a large public was fascinated and horrified by the mysterious character of these assassins and their motives. But closer examination of the phenomenon shows that although a few of the attackers were anarchists, they all acted on their own, without the knowledge and support of the groups to which they belonged. Terrorism was regarded as a wholly new phenomenon, and it was conveniently forgotten that political murder had a very long history. (In France there had been countless attempts to murder Napoleon and Napoleon III in an age well before the rise of anarchism.) However psychologically interesting, this *ère des attentats*, as it was called, was of no great political consequence. By 1905, the wave of attacks and assassinations had abated, and though there were still a few isolated occurrences in Paris and London (for example the Bonnot gang and Peter the Painter), these were small criminal or semicriminal gangs. The era had come to an end.

During the years of World War I, few terrorist acts took place; one of the exceptions was the assassination of the Austrian chancellor Graf Stuergkh by a leading socialist, a dramatic form of protest against the war and against a not altogether appropriate target. By and large, individual terror seemed pointless at a time when millions of people were being killed on the battlefields. Under those circumstances the death of a politician, however prominent, would hardly attract much attention.

AFTER WORLD WAR I

Until the First World War, terrorism was thought to be mainly left wing in ideology. This assessment was dubious even at the time; it was certainly not true with regard to the postwar period and it was not true before 1914, given the highly individualistic character of the small terrorist groups. One could not possibly consider the Irish patriots, the Armenians, the Macedonians, or the Bengali partisans of the left.

One group, the Black Hundred, which appeared in Russia soon after the turn of the century, was certainly terrorist in character; however, its avowed aim was not to help the revolutionaries but to combat them. It engaged in anti-Jewish pogroms and killed some of the liberal leaders of the day. It was decidedly chauvinist, but it also adopted some populist demands. It certainly did not belong to the left, but it was not on the right, either. It represented a right-wing movement of a new type, something like a halfway house on the road toward fascism.

Generalizations with regard to terrorism are almost always misleading, but it can be said that terrorism in the 1920s and 1930s certainly stemmed more from the extreme right than the left. A typical example was the German Freikorps, small bands of ex-soldiers and students who had been too young to fight in the war. They wanted to defend the fatherland against foreign and domestic dangers; their most prominent victims were, in 1919, Rosa Luxemburg and Karl Liebknecht, the heroes and martyrs of the abortive German revolution, and the German foreign minister, Walther Rathenau, in 1922.

There were some terrorist operations in the early history of Italian fascism. Mussolini gave support to the extreme right-wing Croatian Ustasha. The Ustasha wanted independence for their country, and like many other terrorists, they welcomed help from any quarter. Their most striking operation was the dual murder of King Alexander of Yugoslavia and French prime minister Barthou as they met in Marseilles in April 1934.

The Rumanian Iron Guard (formerly the Legion of the Archangel Michael), a political party of the far right, engaged in terrorism, as did other similar movements in Eastern Europe, the Balkans, and the Middle East. The Irgun in Palestine, a country that was administered by Britain at the time, came into being in the late 1930s as the armed wing of the right-wing Revisionist Party. A few anarchists continued to be active in the 1920s where they had been traditionally strong (as in Spain), and the Communists also engaged on various occasions in terrorist operations (such as in Bulgaria in 1923 when they blew up the Sofia cathedral). But by and large, the interwar period witnessed little traditional terrorism, because this was the age of mass political parties on both right and left and of state terrorism.

While fascism and communism firmly subscribed to violence, they stood for collective rather than individual terrorism. In the case of communism, an ideological justification had been given by Lenin, who did not reject terrorism in principle but thought it in most cases harmful and counterproductive. Terrorism, Lenin wrote, was one form of the military struggle that might be usefully applied or even be essential during certain moments of battle. In October 1905, during the last phase of the Russian Revolution, he said that he regretted that his party only talked about making bombs but had never actually produced one. Some leading Marxists at the time rejected terrorism as a matter of principle, and others, such as Trotsky, were against it for pragmatic reasons. Even if successful, he wrote in 1911, terrorism would only cause confusion among the ruling classes for a short time. The capitalist system did not rest on a government minister and would not disappear with the eradication of one.

AFTER WORLD WAR II

With the end of the Second World War, the terrorist action shifted from Europe to the Middle East and Asia. There was no neo-Nazi or neo-fascist terrorism in the years after 1945, as many had feared; with the defeat of the Axis powers, the fanatical enthusiasm had vanished. In Eastern Europe and the Balkans, including those areas in which terrorism had been endemic, the presence of the Red Army and, later on, the heavy hand of the local secret police were sufficient to act as a deterrent. Even in Spain, one of the classic sites of terrorism, neither anarchists nor Basque separatists dared challenge the military dictatorship. Spanish anarchism was no longer a vital force, and the Basques had to wait for the relative freedom that followed Franco's death to resume their activities.

But in the colonies and other dependencies in North Africa and the Middle East, violent campaigns were launched by nationalist groups striving for independence. Terrorist acts had, of course, taken place before in the East, for example, prime ministers had been assassinated in Iraq and Egypt. But with the weakening of the colonial powers, violence gained a new, powerful momentum.

In predominantly agrarian societies, this usually took the form of guerrilla warfare, with China and Indochina as the classic examples, but the emergence of the terrorist Mau-Mau in Kenya and the activity of the Malayan insurgents (mainly Chinese) are others. In urban societies such as Palestine and Cyprus, the action, by necessity, took place mainly in the cities. In Algeria, the struggle against the French proceeded both in the cities and in the countryside, and elements of terrorism and guerrilla warfare appeared side by side.

Terrorism in Palestine, spearheaded by Irgun, had first appeared on the eve of the Second World War, but then Irgun called an armistice and some of its members joined the British forces. However, even before the war ended, the group renewed its attacks against the mandated power. A smaller, even more radical offshoot, the Stern Gang (Fighters for the Freedom of Israel), had attacked ceaselessly, and their leader was hunted down and shot by the British police in Tel Aviv in 1942. The politics of the Stern Gang were more than a little confused; in the early phase of the war they had looked for cooperation from the Italians and even the Germans, and later on they were attracted to Soviet communism. Their anti-imperialist manifestos often read as if they had been composed in Moscow. But their left-wing motivation was not deeply rooted. Both Irgun and the Stern Gang dissolved after the state of Israel came into being, and leading members of the Stern Gang were arrested following the murder of Count Bernadotte, the Swedish mediator, in 1948. The leader of Irgun, Menachem Begin, and one of the leaders of the Stern Gang, Yitzhak Shamir, in later years became prime ministers of Israel. These are just two examples of the many cases of guerrilla or terrorist leaders having a second, political career after their fighting days were over.

The Algerian war for independence began in 1954 in the mountainous regions of the country, was carried to the cities, and lasted for seven years. The terrorist part of the campaign was not too successful—the French smashed the rebel FLN cadres in the capital and the campaign did not go well in the countryside. But the rebels had the great advantage of having sanctuaries in the neighboring countries. Twenty thousand of their fighters were assembled outside the reach of the French, who gradually lost the stomach for making the effort needed to keep the renitent country under its control.

As in Israel, the terrorist campaigns were followed by decades of peace, but eventually radical elements again asserted themselves. This led to the second Algerian war in the 1990s and, in Israel, the murder of Prime Minister Rabin in 1995.

Generally speaking, Middle Eastern politics remained violent, marked by the assassination of a great many leaders—among them King Abdullah of Jordan in 1951 and Anwar Sadat of Egypt in 1981—and a variety of Syrian, Lebanese, and Iranian government ministers. After the emergence of radical Muslim elements, terrorism became even more rampant. Political assassinations, needless to say, occurred in many other parts of Asia and Africa. The murder of Gandhi in 1948, and in later years of Indira Gandhi and Rajiv, her son who succeeded her as prime minister, are particularly striking examples. But it was above all in the Muslim countries of North Africa and the Middle East that systematic and sustained terrorism prevailed in the 1950s, even before anti-Israeli terrorism became a major and well-publicized feature of world politics in the 1960s. Third World terrorism was, almost without exception, inspired by nationalism or political religion.

LATIN AMERICAN TERRORISM

In Latin America, there was a recurrence of terrorism in the late 1960s that was not nationalist-separatist in character but drew its inspiration from the extreme left. The Tupamaros of Uruguay were the prototype of this new terrorism. They emerged in a country that for years had been the most progressive in Latin America, and even in the 1960s was among the more liberal. The Tupamaros, who stood for radical political and social change, attracted some of the best and most idealistic from the younger generation, and they engaged in bank robberies and kidnappings but not in indiscriminate murder. Initially their activities were quite successful, proving that a civilian government could be easily disrupted. The Tupamaros attracted a great deal of attention in the world media, but in the final analysis the only result of their operations was the destruction of freedom in a country that almost alone in Latin America had an unbroken democratic tradition, however imperfect. The campaign of the Tupamaros caused the rise of a military dictatorship and destroyed the democratic system and, at the same time, brought about the destruction of their own movement. By the 1970s, the remaining Tupamaros were in exile bemoaning the evil doings of an oppressive regime they themselves had helped to bring to power. The grave diggers of liberal Uruguay, as Regis Debray later wrote, had also dug their own graves. Facing defeat, the Tupamaros tried their hand at establishing a united front of the left together with nonterrorist parties, but they fared badly in popular elections.

Terrorism in Argentina began a few years after the outbreak in Uruguay. It was on a far more massive scale, and both the terrorist operations and the backlash were more indiscriminate and bloody. In contrast to their Uruguayan comrades, Argentinian terrorists consisted of two groups: the Montoneros (basically Peronist in orientation and social composition) and the smaller but better-equipped and organized ERP (more doctrinally left-wing in character, consisting mainly of students). The Montoneros, who had the whole Peronist left wing as a base of recruitment, began their campaign with the killing of ex-President Aramburu in May 1971. Initially, a considerable number of foreigners (or locals representing foreign economic interests) were among the victims, but gradually the terrorism turned against the army, the police, politicians, and moderate union leaders. There were also a great many unintended victims who died because they happened to be where bombs exploded.

Terrorism in Argentina reached its height in the period 1975–76. There were 646 political murders in 1976, and the terrorists attacked military installations in some provincial cities. Argentina is perhaps the only recorded example of urban guerrilla activity—that is, where terrorists came close to establishing liberated zones in urban areas. But the terrorists overreached precisely because they engaged in large-scale operations that made it easier for the army to combat them. Once the army received a free hand to retaliate, no mercy was shown. Four thousand members of the Montoneros and the ERP were detained, thousands more were arrested, and many were tortured or disappeared without a trace, including many innocent people. Thus, a terrible price was paid for the ill-conceived terrorist campaign. True, within a decade military dictatorship in Argentina, as in Uruguay, gave way to a civilian government that gradually became more democratic, but the experience of these countries did show that even weak and ineffective governments were capable of defending themselves when terrorists had no hope of gaining the support of significant sections of the population.

Latin America deserves mention here because of the strategy of its so-called urban guerrillas, despite the fact that guerrilla activities here were short-lived. Abraham Guillen, a refugee from Spain, advocated guerrilla cells consisting of no more than five or six members who would be constantly on the move. But in his writings Guillen also suggested stronger political action, and clandestine existence and constant mobility was not possible in combination with open political propaganda. And there were the writings of Brazilian Carlos Marighella, who had been a member of the Communist Party but left it because it had been too tame for his taste; he was probably more widely read among his European admirers than in his native country. His "mini-manual" was translated into many languages, but his advocacy of a scorched earth, sabotage of transport and oil pipelines, and destruction of food supplies was quite unrealistic. Marighella assumed that the masses would blame the authorities for these disasters, but the masses were less naive than he thought. Even among the extremists, not many accepted his strategy.

These terrorist theories can be lumped into an approach called the strategy of provocation, an approach that had failed everywhere else. The strategy was based on the assumption that violence would produce repression, which would generate more revolutionary violence, which in turn would provoke yet more draconian measures by the government, which would shatter its "liberal facade." Eventually society would be totally polarized, and in the confrontation between the left and the right, the extreme left was bound to win. The strategy was based on the tacit assumption that the intelligentsia, especially the students, represented the revolutionary vanguard, even though lip service was almost always paid to the crucial role of workers and peasants.

As Latin American terrorists later admitted, the strategy overestimated the strength of the terrorists and underestimated the forces of repression. If the terrorists succeeded in frightening off the police, usually weak and ill equipped, this merely resulted in their having to face the army, which was not hampered by state regulations and laws and could use repressive measures, including torture, as they saw fit. The Brazilian "urban guerrilla" campaign lasted three years, but it never reached the intensity seen in Uruguay and Argentina. It ended with Marighella being shot in a police ambush in São Paulo in November 1969, and the other terrorist commanders eliminated in similar circumstances.

The police in Latin American countries used systematic torture against terrorists, but it is also true that the terrorists had not shown an excess of humanity in their operations: agricultural workers were killed because they had stumbled on an arms cache or hideouts; motorists were murdered because the terrorists needed their cars; and boatmen were cut down after a getaway at gunpoint. These and similar deeds did not add to the popularity of the terrorists. It is useful to recall that Castro and the Cubans had foreseen some of these difficulties. Keeping in mind not only the obstacles of operating in cities but the temptation to excess, they called urban terrorism the "grave of the revolutionaries."

Most Latin American countries witnessed urban terror, and it would be tedious to survey all of them here. Venezuela was one of the first to confront urban terrorism, and in some respects the country seemed predestined for it, since two-thirds of the population lived in urban centers and a substantial part of the powerful Communist Party supported the terrorists. (This was a fairly rare exception, because relations between terrorists and Communists were usually not good; the Communists considered the terrorists dangerous adventurers far from the spirit of Marxism-Leninism, whereas the terrorists saw the Communists as no better than other conservative politicians who talked much and did little.) Terrorism in Venezuela failed not because of massive police repression— the measures taken by the democrat Betancourt were halfhearted—but because the terrorists caused more irritation and hardship for the general public than for the government, disrupted daily life, and brought about a public groundswell of revulsion against themselves.

Neither was terrorism very successful at the time in Colombia, even though this country had one of the most violent political traditions in Latin America: The terrorist movement M 19 appeared on the scene not when repression was most violent but, on the contrary, when a democratically elected government had taken over and when economic development was strong. In later years there was to be a resurgence of terrorism in Colombia, but this had more to do with the appearance of the drug cartels and their growing power than with revolutionary zeal.

LEFT-WING TERRORISM IN GERMANY AND ITALY

A new wave of terrorism of left-wing inspiration appeared in Europe in the late 1960s, partly in the wake of the student revolt of 1968. The German "Red Army" (the Baader Meinhof group) was active for about seven years, and it was succeeded by the movements "June 2nd" and the "Red Cells." According to Red Army ideology, this group was the vanguard of the exploited and oppressed Third World, terrorism being the only feasible strategy of weak revolutionary movements. But the Third World they invoked was a figment of their imagination, and if it had existed, it would not have wanted any part of these three dozen young men and women who called themselves an "army," and who lived in a world of infantile dreams.

The Baader Meinhof group was middle class by origin, which they regarded as a blemish. They tried to compensate for the absence of a proletarian background by the frequent use of four-letter words. There is reason to believe that some of its leading members were to some degree mentally unstable: Baader was heavily dependent on drugs, and Meinhof had suffered some brain damage earlier in her life. Their later suicides also tend to point in this direction. There were more women than men in the ranks of this group, and the women were often more fanatical.

Over the years the Red Army attacked several banks, burned a department store or two, and killed a number of bankers, industrialists, and judges. But none of the victims was very prominent, nor could they have been regarded as major enemies, of either Baader Meinhof, of the revolutionary movement, or of the Third World. Their names seem to have been picked out of a telephone directory. One victim, Dr. Drenkmann, the president of a Berlin court, was a Social Democrat who had never had any contact with the Red Army or its supporters.

Initially, the Red Army had hundreds of supporters, some of whom were willing to give active help. But gradually they lost sympathy, as it became obvious that the terrorists were living in a fantasy world and that their ill-conceived actions had no political impact whatsoever, except perhaps to tarnish the image of the left.

If Baader Meinhof had originally been deeply if unrealistically motivated by ideology, the second and third generation of German left-wing terrorists did not tend toward reflection. They engaged in terrorism because their predecessors had done so. If they had a specific political orientation, they were unwilling or unable to express it. A few terrorist acts took place during the 1980s and early 1990s, but by and large these groups had become irrelevant, and even the media, which originally had devoted inordinate attention to their activities, lost interest.

Italian left-wing terrorism was conducted on a considerably wider scale; it was spearheaded by the Brigate Rosse, which came into being in 1970. The inspiration in Italy came less from the New Left, which had never been very strong in that country, and more from radical groups within the Communist Youth League and, to some extent, from the student groups of the left wing of the Christian Democrats, which had undergone a rapid process of radicalization. As the Red Brigades saw it, Italy was not a democratic country but a bourgeois dictatorship; the language of arms was the only language understood by the ruling class. The Communist Party, these young radicals believed, was a reformist party that had lost its belief in revolution and radical fervor. The movement was also helped by a general feeling of discontent with the lack of progress on the domestic front; the social structures had been frozen since the end of the war, and one party had been in power throughout the period. As in Germany, the membership was predominantly middle class with a strong admixture of radical chic—such as the involvement of Giangiacomo Feltrinelli, a leading publisher, who blew himself up in circumstances that remain unclear to this day. There were working-class militants, but not many.

The Red Brigades engaged in some 14,000 terrorist attacks within their first ten years. While some parts of Italy were relatively free of terrorism, Rome and the industrial regions of the north were strongly affected. The legal system was almost paralyzed, since jurors were afraid to fulfill their duty; not all judges were prepared to be heroes, and the police were by and large unprepared to deal with this unprecedented challenge. Nevertheless, the Red Brigades alienated many of their erstwhile well-wishers as the result of their attacks on journalists and union officials, and above all their murder of Aldo Moro, who had been the most leftist of all the Christian Democrat prime ministers. Far from bringing about a weakening of the state apparatus, the abduction and murder of Aldo Moro caused a closing of ranks of all the democratic parties, including, for once, the Communists. The Italian terrorists had always believed that only one more push was needed to overthrow the Christian Democrats. Instead, through their violent, indiscriminate actions, they actually helped them survive politically for another decade.

The Italian Communists showed no sympathy for the terrorists who were indirectly causing harm to their political prospects; ironically, the Red Brigades had received, as emerged later on during their trials, logistical and other help from the Soviet Union through various East European countries. East Germany, too, gave shelter to the German and Italian terrorists and assisted them in other ways.

Gradually, the Italian police and the courts began showing greater sophistication in dealing with the terrorists. By 1982, some 1,400 leftist terrorists were in prison and more than a few of them, the so-called *pentiti*, had recanted. This led to splits in the ranks of the terrorists who had not been arrested. By 1984, only one member of the high command of the Brigades had not been apprehended, and the movement had ceased to exist.

AMERICA AND JAPAN

The upsurge in terrorism of the 1960s was not limited to Europe. It manifested itself in various ways in the United States and Japan. In America, it appeared on the radical fringe of the New Left in groups like the Weathermen. In a largely unconnected development, terrorism found adherents among black militants, above all the Black Panthers. The motives that induced young blacks to join the terrorist scene were quite different from those that made middle-class white students join the Weathermen. The students knew nothing about the problems of the ghetto and about unemployment. They were motivated by a crisis of identity, suburban boredom, and the desire for excitement and action. For them, more often than not terrorism was the cure for personal problems. All this was immersed in intellectual confusion that espoused the idea that almost anything was permitted and denounced the absence of values. But the things the white radicals were saying about the wickedness of American culture were *a fortiori* true of the radicals themselves.

Some of the blacks, like George Jackson, who had studied terrorist literature in prison, had reached the conclusion that the city-based industrial establishment had to be destroyed by creating conditions of "perfect disorder." Jackson was killed trying to escape from prison, and Eldridge Cleaver, who had also advocated "armed struggle," became disillusioned after being exposed to the realities of revolutionary society in Cuba and Algeria. Both men had accepted Mao's dictum that power grew out of the barrel of a gun, and they also thought, which Mao never did, that the lumpenproletariat could be the main revolutionary force in society. But all the black leaders did not quite live up to their own prescriptions; Stokely Carmichael, for instance, a leading figure of the movement, did not join the armed struggle of the lumpenproletariat but retreated to a comfortable existence in South Africa with his wife, a well-known singer, and eventually came to favor political rather than armed struggle.

Contemporary Japanese terrorism, which was limited principally to the Japanese Red Army, reflected native traditions as well as Western influences. Many of the ideological disputations of Japanese terrorists were imported from the West, hut they also invoked the spirit of the samurai. Japanese terrorists hijacked a Japanese aircraft, committed murders, including several of their own comrades, and perpetrated a few acts of sabotage, most notably of a Shell refinery in Singapore and of the French embassy in the Hague. They were also instrumental in the massacre at Lod Airport in Israel, and they collaborated with Carlos, the famous multinational terrorist, as well as the Palestinians, and ultimately found asylum in Lebanon. This being the whole extent of their terrorist activities, the Japanese Red Army was much less dangerous than the Japanese sectarian terrorists of the 1990s, who had a true base inside Japan, which the Red Army never had.

TURKEY AND THE PALESTINIANS

Few countries outside the Communist world were as severely affected by terrorism as Turkey in the 1970s. Terrorist activities in that country had been initially sponsored by the extreme left, partly as the result of the resurgence of terrorism in Europe. But within a few years the extreme right joined the battle, and the situation was further complicated by the massive help provided to terrorists by outside countries. The left received support from Bulgaria and other Eastern bloc countries, the right from Syria and other Arab states. The left operated mainly out of the universities, which served as inviolate bases that the police could not enter, and the right used religious institutions for the same purpose. Since the police were in no position to cope with the situation, martial law was imposed in 1971, and by 1974 law and order was more or less restored and a general amnesty declared.

This turned out to be a costly mistake, because the amnesty enabled many militants to resume terrorist operations; in 1978–79, 2,400 political murders were committed in the country, and there was a danger that open warfare would break out in the streets. The army took over again in October 1980, and within a few days order was restored. More than 730,000 weapons were seized and 75,000 suspects arrested during the year following the army coup. Most of these suspects were soon released, but 24,000 were charged with terrorist offenses.

Most terrorist activity in Turkey took place in the big cities, but it was by no means confined to them. Some experts explained the roots of Turkish terrorism with reference to the rapid urbanization that had caused dislocation and internal tensions. The emergence of shantytowns in the vicinity of the big cities provided a great reservoir of uprooted and dissatisfied elements willing to join the terrorist movements. But closer examination shows that most terrorists of the left were not recruited in this milieu, and it is uncertain that they provided most of the rank and file of the right-wing terrorists. There was dissatisfaction with the gradual democratization that Ataturk had begun, and it was unclear whether Turkish society was ready for democracy. The democratic experiment in Turkey had been a partial success only, and while the country had made economic progress, not everyone had benefited in equal measure.

Turkish terrorism faded out in the late 1970s, but only a few years later a new form of violence appeared, sponsored by the Kurdish minority, mainly in nonurban areas. Terrorist acts were also committed by extreme Islamic groups trying to undo the secular Kemalist reforms that had taken place during the last seventy years of Turkish history.

Palestinian terrorism grew out of the Palestinian resistance movement against Israel. There had been attacks against Israeli settlements since the state came into being, mainly small raids across the border, but it was only after the war of 1967 and the occupation of the West Bank that a major terrorist campaign began. Among its main protagonists were initially two smaller, self-styled Marxist groups: the PFLP (Popular Front for the Liberation of Palestine), headed by Dr. Habash, and the Democratic Front for the Liberation of Palestine, led by Najib Hawatme. It should be stressed, however, that the Marxist-Leninist slogans that at one time appeared prominently in the publications of most nationalist terrorist movements, including the IRA and the Basque ETA, always had to be taken with a pinch of salt. They were a concession to the general zeitgeist. When communism became less fashionable, and eventually altogether unfashionable, the Marxist-Leninist slogans were dropped and the essentially nationalist character of these movements was given open expression.

Eventually the PLO, which was both a political organization and something akin to a guerrilla movement, also opted for terrorism through Black September and other ad hoc groups. The Palestinians engaged in a variety of horrific operations, such as the killing of Israeli athletes at the Munich Olympic Games in 1972 and the blowing up of several jumbo jets at Dawson Field in Jordan in September 1970. But these major operations usually backfired: for example, the Dawson Field incident threatened the existence of Jordan, whereupon Black September was suppressed by the Jordanian army. The Israelis retaliated with counterterror inside Israel and abroad, and the hijacking of planes, which at one time had been a main strategy, was given up.

Palestinian terrorism (which will be discussed in more detail later), although not a success per se, had a great advantage over most other terrorist movements—namely, the support extended by many Arab countries, which created considerable political difficulty for Israel. Eventually this pressure exerted by the Arab states through the major powers, combined with the intifada (which was mass rather than individual violence), brought about concessions from Israel. Israel was also hurt by the enormous publicity given even to very minor terrorist events in Israel as compared with the much more destructive terrorism in Sri Lanka and Algeria, for example. The reason was obvious: the media were concentrated in Jerusalem rather than Sri Lanka or Algeria.

As the terrorism of the extreme left receded into the background or petered out altogether, the nationalist-separatist terrorism that had been mostly dormant since the Second World War experienced a major resurgence beginning in the 1970s.

TERRORISM OLD AND NEW: IRA AND ETA

The new age of terrorism is dawning, but the old terrorism is far from dead, even though it has declined markedly in Europe. An example is provided by the situation in Northern Ireland. Violence in Ireland goes back for centuries, and the memory of the battles of Kinsale (1601) and the Boyne (1690) between Protestants and Catholics is kept alive in Republican circles to this day. Terrorism in Ireland developed in 1968–69 following Catholic and Protestant demonstrations and has not ceased since. The last phase of the Troubles in Northern Ireland began in 1969. The early years of the Troubles (1972–76) were by far the bloodiest. Thereafter the annual number of victims declined to about a third of what it had been in the early years. There were spectacular exploits, such as the murder of Lord Mountbatten, the retired Viceroy of India; the killing of Airey Neave, a minister of the Crown; the placing of bombs in commercial centers of London and Manchester, causing much material damage; and the attempt to kill then Prime Minister Thatcher and the Conservative leadership at their party conference. There were also attacks against British forces in Europe, especially in Germany.

But the IRA could have conducted many more widescale and frequent attacks, given the financial support they received and the arms supply at their disposal. What kept their activities down to relatively low levels? The IRA leadership seems to have realized early on that their campaign against the British would be long, and that if it became too formidable a danger, especially on the British mainland, they would not only turn public opinion against themselves but also invite much sharper and more effective counterblows. Nor could they hope to substantially strengthen their position in their own community; in parliamentary elections they hardly ever scored more than 15 percent of the vote.

Their strategy from the late 1970s on seems to have been to wear out the British, perhaps to await a time when Britain would he in so weak a position that it would have to make concessions it had been reluctant to consider in the past. The aims of the Republicans were, after all, limited in scope compared with those of Palestinian groups such as Hamas. They wanted not the total destruction of their enemy but merely a united Ireland.

Hence the political negotiations that began in 1993. The ground had been prepared in talks between London and Dublin in which constitutional safeguards were laid out. On this basis the IRA declared an armistice in August 1994; the Protestant groups followed suit a month later. The truce lasted until February 1996, when the IRA resumed hostilities. The main bone of contention was the British demand that the IRA surrender its arsenal of arms. This was interpreted by Sinn Fein, the political wing of the IRA, as unilateral disarmament and hence unacceptable.

Multiparty talks went on, but Sinn Fein was excluded as long as the IRA attacks continued. Then, in 1997, Labor came to power in Britain, with the desire to make a new start. Sinn Fein, beset by internal divisions, did not at first respond. The Protestants, on the basis of their past experiences, were reluctant to participate as the new British government renewed negotiations with Sinn Fein in August 1997, with the decommissioning of arms still the main issue at stake. After many setbacks, these talks led to agreement in 1998,

There was the impression that while the old hostility and mutual suspicion continued unabated, a majority of IRA militants were in favor of trying to negotiate a settlement or at least opting for a long truce. But it was also clear that an extremist minority wanted to fight on. These diehards were largely motivated by temperament rather than ideological differences. There was a hard core of younger people (the Irish Continuity Army) who were professional terrorists, just as in an earlier age there had been professional revolutionaries all over Europe. This was their life and the only profession they had learned. What would they do once peace had been established? Hence the decision to kill a leading Protestant terrorist inside the Maze prison in Belfast, which led to a new round of terrorist actions.

Since it was unlikely that in a peaceful settlement all the demands of the extremists would be met, there was reason to assume that at least some terrorists would continue the struggle. This could well be a repeat performance of 1921, when the militants continued to fight after the agreement with London to establish an Irish Free State. They had been subdued only after a civil war, which had set Irish freedom fighters, that era's comrades in arms, against each other. This scenario is, of course, not limited to Ireland; it applies, in all probability, to every terrorist campaign. There always will be some ultras dissatisfied with a political settlement, eager to fight on. But the vote in Northern Ireland in the spring of 1998 showed clearly that the majority of Catholics wanted an end to the armed conflict and that a majority of Protestants, albeit not on the same scale, shared their feelings. And yet the peace agreement was followed by the bloodiest attack in the whole history of the conflict, carried out by a splinter group calling itself the "real IRA." Whether the peace will last cannot be predicted with certainty. But as of this writing in 1999, terrorism in Ireland has come to an end after long negotiations and the intervention of the American president, Bill Clinton, and the British prime minister, Tony Blair.

The parallels between the IRA and the Basque ETA are striking in many respects: both are motivated by enormous enthusiasm, even though the groups constitute only a minority within their own community. Basque opposition against what is perceived as oppression by the Madrid centralists goes back to the nineteenth century and possibly even further.

Basque nationalism was effectively suppressed under General Franco, and while the first acts of sabotage took place when Franco was still alive (the derailment of a railway in 1961), a major campaign started only after the dictator had died and most of the Basque militants had been released from prison. Admiral Carrero Blanco, Franco's successor, was assassinated, and in 1979 there were eighty-two political murders, eighty-eight the year after. Basque terrorism, despite setbacks, continued up to the fall of 1998, albeit on a smaller scale than before.

The ETA has achieved considerable political concessions, but this success has not been remotely sufficient to satisfy the nationalists. The aim of the extremists remains an independent Basque state. But given the demographic realities, especially the fact that the Basque are a minority in their own region, this can be achieved only by ethnic cleansing, the exodus of the non-Basques, or their voluntarily becoming Basques. This would mean transforming the war against the Spanish government into a war against the Spanish people and also eventually against the majority of Basques who do not subscribe to ETA ideology (semi-Trotskyite in the 1970s and early '80s, and ultranationalist in the 1990s). The political wing of ETA polled 12 percent of the votes in the Basque country in the general elections of 1996, in comparison to 14 percent in the previous elections. From a self-styled anti-colonialist, anti-capitalist, anti-imperialist revolutionary movement, ETA had turned into a purely nationalist movement, one that supported a social program that did not differ substantially from that of other Spanish parties.

The high tide of ETA terrorism came in 1978–80, certainly as far as the number of victims is concerned. After that, though the number of militants may have increased somewhat, the number of assassinations has decreased. Five occurred in 1996 and twelve in 1997, compared to the annual average in 1970–95 of more than twenty. (ETA differs from the IRA in its involvement in kidnapping and extortion, for which the IRA has little appetite.)

ETA's prospects seem dim. It has largely lost its bases in France following an agreement between the French and Spanish governments. There is no goodwill for its cause among Spaniards, and no attempt has been made to generate such goodwill. Nevertheless, ETA still has the support of a fanatical minority in their own region. Eventually, a political solution might be found; this will undoubtedly lead to a split, as in the case of the IRA, since the ultranationalists cannot possibly achieve all they want.

In the Basque region, as in Northern Ireland, a culture of violence has developed over the years that tends to perpetuate itself. It is, in all probability, a generational question. As one generation of professional terrorists ages and by necessity opts out of the armed struggle, a new one may or may not emerge. Or it may appear after an interruption of a few decades, as has happened in Irish history time and again.

A PROFILE OF TERRORISM

Who are the persons behind the masks of terrorist movements? Are there any distinguishing characteristics that can be observed about the individuals or the groups? Terrorist groups have frequently consisted of younger members of the educated middle classes, but there have also been instances of agrarian terrorism and terrorism by the uprooted and rejected in society. In very few exceptions—for example, the Molly Maguires in the United States—there has been working-class terrorism, but it clearly has been the exception.

In nationalist-separatist groups, the middle-class element has usually been less influential than it has been in terrorist cells of the extreme left. Movement of national liberation and social revolution have turned to terrorism after political action failed. But terrorism has also been the first resort, chosen by militant groups impatient for quick results.

Assassinations of leading officials have been tried within modern totalitarian regimes, but the means of repression at the disposal of the totalitarian state have effectively ruled out any systematic terrorism. Terrorism has been infrequent in societies in which violence has not been part of the tradition and political culture, but few parts of the world have been altogether free of it.

National oppression and social inequities are frequently mentioned as the root causes of terrorism, and it is, of course, true that happy, contented groups of people seldom, if ever, throw bombs. But this does not explain why the struggle for political freedom, for national liberation, or for secession has only occasionally led to terrorism, and why certain national minorities have opted for terrorism and others have not—why, for instance, the Basque militants have engaged in a long terrorist campaign, whereas the Catalan have not. History shows it has little to do with the severity of the oppression measured by any acceptable standard; terrorism is largely a matter of perception, of historical, social, and cultural traditions, and of political calculus.

Generalizations about terrorism are difficult for yet another reason. Terrorist groups are usually small; some are very small indeed. While historians and sociologists can sometimes account for mass movements, the movements of small particles in politics, as in physics, often defies explanation. Some of the most striking assassinations in history, including that of U.S. president Kennedy, were carried out by lone individuals rather than groups; the investigation of their motives belongs to the realm of psychology rather than politics.

Having said this, some general statements can be made about the mainsprings of terrorism, its strategy, and its tactics. Seldom, if ever, have terrorists assumed that they would be able to seize power outright—most believe in the strategy of provocation. The Irish believed that their attacks would lead to counterterrorism, that, as a result, the fighting spirit of Ireland would reawaken, and, in the end, that Britain would have to make concessions. The Russian revolutionaries decided to kill the German ambassador to Moscow and the German governor in Kiev in 1918, assuming that this would lead to a resumption of hostilities between the young Soviet regime and Imperial Germany. In a similar way, the Armenian terrorists before 1914 and the Palestinian terrorists after 1967 aimed at bringing about foreign intervention,

The choice of victims is often arbitrary; while the Russian terrorists concentrated their attacks in the beginning against tsarist officials who had shown particular brutality, later terrorists, on the contrary, killed moderate political leaders who they thought were more dangerous political enemies. Two examples already mentioned are the murder of Walther Rathenau, the German foreign minister, in 1922, and the Italian politician Aldo Moro; a third is Grand Duke Franz Ferdinand of Austria, who was killed by Serbian terrorists precisely because he had the reputation of a liberal willing to make concessions.

On a few occasions, terrorists achieved their aims. Count Orsini was acting on his own when he carried out his spectacular bomb attack in Paris in 1857, but it pushed Napoleon III to decide to give the Italians military assistance against Austria. Orsini would not have succeeded unless Napoleon had favored such a policy in any case. When terrorism has been successful, it has usually been because the terrorist demands were limited and clearly defined. That the wages of American ironworkers more than doubled between 1905 and 1910 was at least in part connected with the fact that during this period about one hundred buildings and bridges were bombed. Alternatively, systematic terror has been successful when carried out within the framework of a wider strategy. Thus, the Vietcong killed some 10,000 village elders in the late 1950s and early 1960s, and the Algerian FLN systematically killed their political rivals, the followers of Messali Haj, as a prologue to a wider and more ambitious strategy.

Many terrorist groups have without hesitation attacked the police and, of course, civilians, but have shown reluctance to attack the military. They must have assumed that the military would be a harder target and that there would be massive retaliation.

Terrorism has evolved in fits and starts. Forms of extremist violence appear and then slowly dissolve, giving rise to new variations which likewise come and go in due time. In this sense, there have been many different versions of terrorism in history, each one distinguished by its unique ends and means. No two types have ever been quite the same. Interestingly, each imparts some aspect of itself to those that follow. As one kind of terrorism fades into the past, it leaves behind a residue that, to a greater or lesser extent, is incorporated into its successors, shaping their development. No form of terrorism, current or past, has operated in a vacuum. Common wisdom might hold that extremist violence is unique to one particular place in time, and in some ways it is; yet in its essence, terror is part of a historical process in which the old informs the new.

This process, whereby a grim inheritance is passed down from one historical terrorism to another, moves forward at regular intervals or, as the next author claims, in waves. Indeed, as David C. Rappaport wrote in late 2001, terrorism's evolution, at least since the late nineteenth century, has proceeded in waves—four, to be precise. According to Rappaport, the world today is experiencing the fourth terrorist wave, one that began in 1979 and continues into the present. Its three predecessors, he claims, left ideological, organizational, and operational legacies that have made the fourth wave all the more dangerous. In the next essay, Rappaport contends that this cumulative function of terrorism will make combating it a vastly more difficult task than most people imagine. Each successive wave has refined and strengthened the next, adding force that generates ever-greater destructive energy. The world, as a result, is threatened mightily by this new fourth wave of terror.

The Fourth Wave: September 11 in the History of Terrorism
DAVID C. RAPOPORT

September 11 marks the most important date in the long and bloody history of terrorism. No other terrorist attack used passenger planes as bombs, produced such staggering casualty figures, created such enormous universal outrage, and galvanized such a wide response, one that could reshape the character of international relations. But even this act of terror should be studied in the context of the history of terrorism—a history that demonstrates how deeply implanted terrorism has become in modern culture during the last two centuries, and suggests how and why its face changes.

THE WAVES OF TERROR

Terrorism has a long and significant history in various religious traditions. But the concept as distinguished from the phenomena is a recent development, a feature of the French Revolution. When the term entered our language in 1795, terrorism was seen as the indispensable tool to establish a democratic order: "virtue or the terror," Robespierre proclaimed.

The practices of the revolutionary tribunals exemplified the purpose and method. Ordinary courts assessed the behavior of defendants, but the revolutionary tribunals examined the "hearts" of suspects and found it necessary to scrap the ordinary rules of evidence as impediments to accomplishing the new task. Conventional notions of guilt and innocence became irrelevant. Justice was not the issue; the problem was how to publicize a prisoner's fate to serve as a didactic lesson by identifying appropriate and inappropriate civic character traits.

Nearly a century later, the first terror rebel movement, Narodnaya Volya (The People's Will), emerged in 1879, and its successors haunted Russia for nearly four decades. Seeking a radical transformation of society, the group's members understood terrorism as a temporary necessity to "raise the consciousness of the masses" and selected victims for symbolic reasons—that is, for the emotional and political responses their deaths would have. Their objectives were never achieved, but their influence endured to generate a "culture of terror" for successors to inherit and improve.

The uniqueness of Narodnaya Volya should be emphasized. It had successful predecessors: the Sons of Liberty in the American war for independence tarred and feathered loyalists, forcing many to leave the country, and the KKK ended the Reconstruction period by causing federal troops to withdraw from the south. But neither group gave others a strategy to ponder; they did their dirty work in secret and kept their mouths shut afterward.

The doctrine of Russian rebel terror involved extranormal acts of violence or acts designed to violate conventions that regulate violence, namely rules of war that enable one to distinguish between combatant and noncombatant. The Russians called themselves terrorists rather than guerrillas precisely because guerrilla targets were military and theirs were not. A new form of publicity was necessary because spontaneous mass uprisings had become impossible, and revolutionaries were known as "idle word-spillers." Terror would command the masses' attention, arouse latent political tensions, and provoke government to respond indiscriminately, undermining in the process its own credibility and legitimacy. Successful terror entailed learning how to fight and how to die; the most admirable death occurred as a result of a court trial at which the terrorist accepted responsibility for an assassination and used the occasion to indict the regime. The terrorist, Stepniak wrote "is noble, terrible, irresistibly fascinating, uniting the two sublimities of human grandeur, the martyr and the hero."

Since the 1880s, four successive, overlapping, major waves of terror have washed over the world, each with its own special character, purposes, and tactics.[1] The first three lasted approximately a generation each; and the fourth, which began in 1979, is still in process. Sometimes, organizations created in one wave survived when the wave bringing it ebbed. (The Irish Republican Army, or IRA, for example, began in the anticolonial wave in the 1920s.)

Major unexpected political turning points exposing new government vulnerabilities precipitated each wave. Hope was excited, and hope is always an indispensable lubricant of rebel activity, making the discontented active and the transfer of legitimacy away from government possible.

Ironically, the first wave was stimulated by massive political and economic reforms introduced by the czars. Hopes were aroused but could not be fulfilled quickly enough; and in the wake of inevitable disappointment, systematic assassination campaigns against prominent officials began. Dynamite, a recent invention, was the weapon of choice, and the bomb the terrorist threw distinguished him from the ordinary criminal because it usually killed the terrorist too, an event more effectively dramatized in a period that saw the rise of the mass daily newspaper.

An Armenian movement developed and the Balkans exploded, as many groups (the Internal Macedonian Revolutionary Organization, Young Bosnia, and the Serbian Black Hand) found the boundaries of states that had been recently torn out of the Ottoman Empire unsatisfactory. In the West, revolutionary Anarchists mounted assassination campaigns to frustrate drives toward universal suffrage, a reform they thought would make existing political systems invulnerable. But the first wave dried up largely when the Austrian archduke's assassination precipitated World War I.

The second wave began in the 1920s and crested in the 1960s. Oddly, its principal stimulus was a major war aim of the victorious allies in both world wars: national self-determination. The ambivalence of colonial powers about their own legitimacy made them ideal targets for a politics of atrocity. A variety of new states—including Ireland, Israel, Cyprus, Yemen, and Algeria—emerged, and the wave receded largely as colonial powers disappeared. Different and more useful targets were chosen. Martyrdom seemed less important, and so prominent political figures were not targets. Instead, the police forces, a government's "eyes and ears," were decimated by assassination campaigns, and their military replacements seemed too clumsy to cope without producing counteratrocities, which generated greater social support for the terrorists. If the process of atrocities and counteratrocities were well planned, they worked nearly always to favor those perceived to be weak and without alternatives.

In cities, the terrorists developed cellular structures almost impervious to police penetration. Major energies went into guerrilla-like hit-and-run actions against troops, attacks that went beyond the rules of war because weapons were concealed and the assailants had no identifying insignia. Some groups (Irgun in Palestine and the IRA) made efforts, however, to give warnings to limit damage to civilians.

Partly because anticolonial causes were more appealing to outsiders, defining these groups became vexing. The term terrorist had accumulated so many abusive connotations that being identified as such carried enormous political liabilities, and rebels stopped calling themselves terrorists. Lehi (the "Stern Gang"), a Zionist revisionist group, was the last organization to describe its activity as terrorist. Members of Menachem Begin's Irgun, concentrating on purpose rather than means, described themselves as "freedom fighters" who were battling government terror, a description all subsequent groups used. Governments returned the compliment, deeming every rebel who used violence a terrorist. The media corrupted language further, refusing often to use terms consistently to avoid being seen as blatantly partisan. Some developed an extraordinary policy of describing the same individuals in the same account alternatively as terrorists, guerrillas, and soldiers.

The Vietnam war precipitated the third wave as the effectiveness of Vietcong terror against the American Goliath armed with modern technology kindled hopes that the Western heartland was vulnerable too. A revolutionary ethos emerged comparable to that in the initial wave. Many, such as the American Weather Underground, German Red Army Faction, Italian Red Brigades, and French Direct Action, saw themselves as vanguards for the masses of the third world, a view the Soviet Union encouraged covertly.

Occasionally, a revolutionary ethos and separatist purpose were linked (for example, the Basque Nation and Liberty or ETA, the

lutionary bonds, but groups in separate states did not cooperate and the heroes invoked in their literature were almost always national ones. They seemed to understand that a search for an international brotherhood would probably weaken its abilities to make better use of other international resources.

Diaspora groups sometimes displayed abilities not seen in earlier waves. The Israelis received funds, weapons, and volunteers from the Jewish diaspora, and American Jews significantly influenced United States policy. The Algerian National Liberation Front (FLN) received considerable aid from the Arab world, and neighboring Arab states offered sanctuaries and did not prevent their lands from being used as staging grounds for attacks. The Greek government sponsored the Cypriot uprising against the British in the 1950s. The different Irish experiences illustrate how crucial influences are shaped by foreign perceptions of purpose and context. The first effort in the 1920s, seen as anticolonial, gained enormous support from Irish Americans and the United States government, resulting in an Irish state. The supporting parties abandoned the IRA during its brief campaign to gain Northern Ireland in World War II and in the 1950s during the cold war. Although IRA efforts during the 1960s were met more favorably, the early Marxist dimension generated considerable anxiety; not until the cold war was over did the American government show serious interest in the issue again, helping initiate and perhaps resolve the conflict.

The third wave of international terrorism was the shortest because it was too dependent on forces it could not control. The emphasis on the revolutionary bond or the brotherhood of terrorists everywhere alienated potential domestic and liberal constituencies, especially during the cold war. A leader of the German 2d June group once noted that its obsession with the Palestinian cause led the group to put a bomb in a Jewish synagogue on the anniversary of *Kristall Nacht*, a significant Nazi attack on the Jews. This "stupidity," he says, alienated potential German constituencies.

The PLO, which comprises a loose confederation of Palestinian groups, found that the price paid for some international ties was high. Abu Iyad, a founding member and intelligence chief, wrote in the 1970s that because the Palestinian cause was so important in the politics of Arab states, some countries such as Syria and Iraq captured PLO-associated groups to serve their state ends, in effect complicating the enormous PLO divisions. He noted that foreign involvement made it more difficult to settle for a limited goal as the Irgun had done earlier during the Palestine mandate. When a PLO element hijacked British and American planes to Jordan in 1970—the first time non-Israelis were deliberately targeted—the Jordanians, after much bloodshed, forced the PLO to move it base of operations out of Jordan.

To eliminate these problems, states began to sponsor their own terror groups, an activity unknown in the second wave. But the new policy was risky, as events during the 1980s showed. Britain severed diplomatic relations with Libya and Syria for sponsoring terrorism on British soil. France broke relations with Iran when Iran refused to let the French interrogate its embassy staff about the assassination of Iranian émigrés in France. The limited value of state-sponsored terror in this wave is emphasized by Iraqi restraint during the 1990–1991 Persian Gulf war, despite widespread predictions that Iraqi terrorists would flood Europe. Lebanon in the 1980s, however, provided the most successful use of state-sponsored suicide bombing, at least in a strategic sense. The attacks Iran and Syria facilitated compelled most multinational forces to withdraw. But local elements on their own terrain carried out the attacks, which may have inhibited the targeted parties from striking the sponsoring state.

States in this period began to cooperate formally in counterterror efforts. The Americans with British aid bombed Libya in 1986 for state-sponsored terrorist attacks, and the European Community imposed an arms embargo. Two years later some evidence that Libya's agents were involved in the bombing of an American airliner over Lockerbie, Scotland, in 1989 led to a unanimous UN Security Council decision that obliged Libya to extradite the suspects; a decade later Libya complied.

But there were always obstacles to cooperation, even among allies. France refused to extradite PLO, Red Brigade, and ETA suspects to West Germany, Italy, and Spain, respectively. Italy spurned American requests to extradite the Palestinian alleged to have organized the seizure of the Achille Lauro cruise ship in 1984. The United States has refused extradition requests for IRA suspects. In 1988 Italy refused to extradite a Kurd because Turkey might execute him, and Italian law forbids capital punishment. Such events will not stop until the laws and interests of separate states are identical, a virtually unimaginable condition.

Religion, the fourth wave's distinctive characteristic, transcends the state bond. This is a particularly important fact in Islam, where the vast Sunni population is dispersed among so many states and where religious elements are especially active. Obviously, groups from the different mainstream religious traditions do not cooperate and even traditional cleavages within a religion—Shia and Sunni, for example—may be intensified.

The third wave saw the first terrorist organization in history that sought to train and coordinate other terrorist entities, made possible when no effective Lebanese government existed. When Israel expelled the PLO from Lebanon, states hosting the PLO afterward refused to provide facilities to continue the training, and to a large extent, the PLO's career as an effective terrorist organization was over.

The fourth wave's parallel for the PLO is Al Qaeda, but the differences are significant. A weak, friendly Afghan government needs Al Qaeda's aid, one reason why the terrorist training areas are there. Geography conveys enormous advantages in protecting the group: remoteness, mountains, and climate. The PLO trained group members; Al Qaeda trains individuals committed to its goal from various places in the Sunni world, largely in the Middle East. The PLO had a loose divided form while Al Qaeda does seem like a single unit.

THE NEXT WAVES

The September 11 attack has created a resolve in America and elsewhere to end terror everywhere. But the history of terror does not inspire much confidence that this determination will be successful, and problems in sustaining the international coalition appear clearly to mirror problems in past efforts as well.

Terrorism is deeply rooted in modern culture. Even if the fourth wave soon follows the path of its three predecessors, another inspiring cause is likely to emerge unexpectedly, as it has too often in the past. Terrorism's history shows that organizations can be decimated, and useful institutions like ununiformed police forces can be created. It shows that terrorism can be made less significant but terrorists also can invent new ways to carry out their activities. Previous international efforts were difficult to sustain and similar problems are emerging now. Members do not agree on how to apply the term, and the decision not to use it for groups in Kashmir, Lebanon, and Israel demonstrate that the interests of states simply do not sufficiently coincide, and that some will encourage groups others abhor.

Even if the only task is destroying Al Qaeda, formidable problems exist. If American ground troops are required, the experiences of the second wave suggest military forces may have great difficulties. In Cyprus, Jewish Palestine, Algeria, and Ireland, for example, the terrorists were never found, even though the long and costly search was over familiar territory.

The PLO stayed above ground to train foreign terrorists. Perhaps they had to do so, and maybe Al Qaeda must stay above to continue similar operations. Forcing it underground will be no great task, but are we willing let it stay under because the cost of finding it is too great?

NOTES

1. For an earlier and more detailed account of the four waves, see David Rapoport, "Terrorism," in Lester R. Kurtz and Jennifer E. Turpin, eds., *Encyclopedia of Violence, Peace, and Conflict* (London: Academic Press, 1999).

2. Cited in Richard B. Jensen, "The United States, International Policing and the War Against Anarchist Terrorism," *Journal of Terrorism and Political Violence*, vol. 13, no. 1 (Spring 2001), p. 19.

Reprinted with permission from *Current History* magazine (December 2001). © 2007 Current History, Inc.

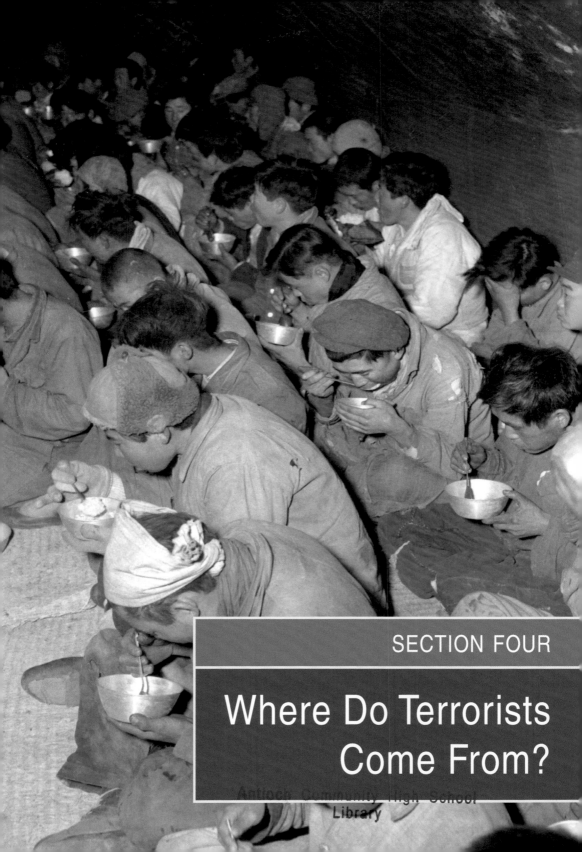

SECTION FOUR

Where Do Terrorists Come From?

Antioch Community High School
Library

It is rather easy to locate either the home countries or bases of operations of today's terrorists. One could point to almost any spot on a map of the world and identify the source of one or another terrorist group. Al Qaeda alone either operates in, has affiliates in, or draws recruits from more than 70 nations, including the United States. Terrorist cells or extremist groups, many connected to at least ideologically to al Qaeda, exist on every continent. Some of the nations that lead in the export of terrorists abroad are Saudi Arabia, Egypt, Yemen, and the semi-autonomous Palestine. Pakistan not only turns out trained terrorist units, but this nominal American ally also supports an Islamic school system that has been associated with the recruitment and indoctrination of future extremists.

The Middle East and South Asia are, of course, rife with terror groups, from Hezbollah and Hamas to Islamic Jihad and the Taliban, but such organizations can be found in Europe and Africa, as well. Europe, for example, is home to the Irish Republican Army and the Basque group ETA, although each has recently declared a ceasefire in its respective conflict. Africa has a vast array of rebel and guerrilla armies, each representing either local or regional movements pushing for political change. The continent's less stable countries, such as Somalia, are also reported to have begun hosting al Qaeda branches, leading many experts to fear that parts of Africa might become a nest of clandestine terrorist training camps.

The Caucasus region south of Russia produces its fair share of violent extremists, as do the Southeast Asian countries of Indonesia and the Philippines. Even the United States contributes an occasional domestic or international terrorist into the global pool of ready and willing killers. No one place on the globe, then, can claim a monopoly on the production and distribution of terrorists.

The search area, however, can be narrowed down dramatically if one draws a distinction between the extremists' home countries and the places from which they emerge fully trained and mission-ready. In this case, one needs to look for chaotic, war-torn lands, brimming with opportunities to hone such skills as assassination, kidnapping, and suicide bombing. Here, Afghanistan and Iraq take center stage. Both function as veritable terrorist boot camps, where operatives practice the lethal repertoire they will later use elsewhere. Ironically, as Peter Bergen and Alec Reynolds demonstrate in the next article, the United States has helped to create in these places conditions favorable to the production of the very terrorists who so hate the West.

Blowback Revisited: Today's Insurgents in Iraq Are Tomorrow's Terrorists
PETER BERGEN AND ALEC REYNOLDS

When the United States started sending guns and money to the Afghan mujahideen in the 1980s, it had a clearly defined Cold War purpose: helping expel the Soviet army, which had invaded Afghanistan in 1979. And so it made sense that once the Afghan jihad forced a Soviet withdrawal a decade later, Washington would lose interest in the rebels. For the international mujahideen drawn to the Afghan conflict, however, the fight was just beginning. They opened new fronts in the name of global jihad and became the spearhead of Islamist terrorism. The seriousness of the blowback became clear to the United States with the 1993 bombing of the World Trade Center: all of the attack's participants either had served in Afghanistan or were linked to a Brooklyn-based fund-raising organ for the Afghan jihad that was later revealed to be al Qaeda's de facto U.S. headquarters. The blowback, evident in other countries as well, continued to increase in intensity throughout the rest of the decade, culminating on September 11, 2001.

The current war in Iraq will generate a ferocious blowback of its own, which—as a recent classified CIA assessment predicts—could be longer and more powerful than that from Afghanistan. Foreign volunteers fighting U.S. troops in Iraq today will find new targets around the world after the war ends. Yet the Bush administration, consumed with managing countless crises in Iraq, has devoted little time to preparing for such long-term consequences. Lieutenant General James Conway, the director of operations on the Joint Staff, admitted as much when he said in June that blowback "is a concern, but there's not much we can do about it at this point in time." Judging from the experience of Afghanistan, such thinking is both mistaken and dangerously complacent.

COMING HOME TO ROOST

The foreign volunteers in Afghanistan saw the Soviet defeat as a victory for Islam against a superpower that had invaded a Muslim country. Estimates of the number of foreign fighters who fought in Afghanistan begin in the low thousands; some spent years in combat, while others came only for what amounted to a jihad vacation. The jihadists gained legitimacy and prestige from their triumph both within the militant community and among ordinary Muslims, as well as the confidence to carry their jihad to other countries where they believed Muslims required assistance. When veterans of the guerrilla campaign returned home with their experience, ideology, and weapons, they destabilized once-tranquil countries and inflamed already unstable ones.

Algeria had seen relatively little terrorism for decades, but returning mujahideen founded the Armed Islamic Group (known by its French initials, GIA). GIA murdered thousands of Algerian civilians during the 1990s as it attempted to depose the government and replace it with an Islamist regime, a goal inspired by the mujahideen's success in Afghanistan. The GIA campaign of violence became especially pronounced after the Algerian army mounted a coup in 1992 to preempt an election that Islamists were poised to win.

In Egypt, after the assassination of Egyptian President Anwar Sadat in 1981 prompted a government crackdown, hundreds of extremists left the country to train and fight in Afghanistan. Those militants came back from the war against the Soviets to lead a terror campaign that killed more than a thousand people between 1990 and 1997. Closely tied to these militants was the Egyptian cleric Sheikh Omar Abdel Rahman, "the Blind Sheikh," whose preaching, according to the 9/11 Commission, had inspired Sadat's assassins. Abdel Rahman's career demonstrates the internationalization of Islamist extremism after Afghanistan. The cleric visited Pakistan to lend his support to the Afghan jihad and encouraged two of his sons to fight in the war. He also provided spiritual direction for the Egyptian terrorist organization Jamaat al-Islamiyya and supported its renewed attacks on the Egyptian government in the 1990s. He arrived in the United States in 1990—at the time, the country was regarded as a sympathetic environment for Islamist militants—where he began to encourage attacks on New York City landmarks. Convicted in 1995 in connection with the 1993 bombing of the World Trade Center, Abdel Rahman is serving a life sentence in the United States. But his influence has continued to be felt: a 1997 attack at an archaeological site near the Egyptian city of Luxor that left 58 tourists dead and almost crippled Egypt's vital tourism industry was an effort by Jamaat al-Islamiyya to force his release.

The best-known alumnus of the Afghan jihad is Osama bin Laden, under whose leadership the "Afghan Arabs" prosecuted their war beyond the Middle East into the United States, Africa, Europe, and Southeast Asia. After the Soviet defeat, bin Laden established a presence in Sudan to build up his fledgling al Qaeda organization. Around the same time, Saddam Hussein invaded Kuwait and hundreds of thousands of U.S. troops arrived in Saudi Arabia. The U.S. military presence in "the land of the two holy places" became al Qaeda's core grievance, and the United

States became bin Laden's primary target. Al Qaeda bombed two U.S. embassies in Africa in 1998, nearly sank the U.S.S. Cole in Yemen in 2000, and attacked the World Trade Center and the Pentagon in 2001. Bin Laden expanded his reach into Southeast Asia with the assistance of other terrorists who had fought in Afghanistan, such as Riduan Isamuddin, known as Hambali, who is the central link between al Qaeda and the Indonesian terror group Jemaah Islamiyah, and Ali Gufron, known as Mukhlas, a leading planner of the 2002 Bali bombing that killed more than 200 people.

ON-THE-JOB TRAINING

The Afghan experience was important for the foreign "holy warriors" for several reasons. First, they gained battlefield experience. Second, they rubbed shoulders with like-minded militants from around the Muslim world, creating a truly global network. Third, as the Soviet war wound down, they established a myriad of new jihadist organizations, from al Qaeda to the Algerian GIA to the Filipino group Abu Sayyaf.

However, despite their grandiose rhetoric, the few thousand foreigners who fought in Afghanistan had only a negligible impact on the outcome of that war. Bin Laden's Afghan Arabs began fighting the Soviet army only in 1986, six years after the Soviet invasion. It was the Afghans, drawing on the wealth of their American and Saudi sponsors, who defeated the Soviet Union. By contrast, foreign volunteers are key players in Iraq, far more potent than the Afghan Arabs ever were.

Several factors could make blowback from the Iraq war even more dangerous than the fallout from Afghanistan. Foreign fighters started to arrive in Iraq even before Saddam's regime fell. They have conducted most of the suicide bombings—including some that have delivered strategic successes such as the withdrawal of the UN and most international aid organizations—and the Jordanian Abu Musab al-Zarqawi, another alumnus of the Afghan war, is perhaps the most effective insurgent commander in the field. Fighters in Iraq are more battle hardened than the Afghan Arabs, who fought demoralized Soviet army conscripts. They are testing themselves against arguably the best army in history, acquiring skills in their battles against coalition forces that will be far more useful for future terrorist operations than those their counterparts learned during the 1980s. Mastering how to make improvised explosive devices or how to conduct suicide operations is more relevant to urban terrorism than the conventional guerrilla tactics used against the Red Army. U.S. military commanders say that techniques perfected in Iraq have been adopted by militants in Afghanistan.

Finally, foreign involvement in the Iraqi conflict will likely lead some Iraqi nationals to become international terrorists. The Afghans were glad to have Arab money but were culturally, religiously, and psychologically removed from the Afghan Arabs; they neither joined al Qaeda nor identified with the Arabs' radical theology. Iraqis, however, are closer culturally to the foreigners fighting in Iraq, and many will volunteer to continue other jihads even after U.S. troops depart.

IN BAGHDAD AND IN BOSTON

President George W. Bush and others have suggested that it is better for the United States to fight the terrorists in Baghdad than in Boston. It is a comforting notion, but it is wrong on two counts. First, it posits a finite number of terrorists who can be lured to one place and killed. But the Iraq war has expanded the terrorists' ranks: the year 2003 saw the highest incidence of significant terrorist attacks in two decades, and then, in 2004, astonishingly, that number tripled. (Secretary of Defense Donald Rumsfeld famously complained in October 2003 that "we lack metrics to know if we are winning or losing the global war on terror." An exponentially rising number of terrorist attacks is one metric that seems relevant.) Second, the Bush administration has not addressed the question of what the foreign fighters will do when the war in Iraq ends. It would be naive to expect them to return to civilian life in their home countries. More likely, they will become the new shock troops of the international jihadist movement.

For these reasons, U.S. allies in Europe and the Middle East, as well as the United States itself, are vulnerable to blowback. Disturbingly, some European governments are already seeing some of their citizens and resident aliens answer the call to fight in Iraq. In February, the Los Angeles Times reported that U.S. troops in Iraq had detained three French militants—and that police in Paris had arrested ten associates who were planning to join them. In June, authorities in Spain arrested 16 men, mostly Moroccans, on charges of recruiting suicide bombers for Iraq. In September, prosecutors in the United States indicted a Dutch resident, Iraqi-born Wesam al-Delaema, for conspiring to bomb U.S. convoys in Fallujah. These incidents presage danger not only for European countries, but also for the United States, since European nationals benefit from the Visa Waiver Program, which affords them relatively easy access to the United States.

But it is Saudi Arabia that will bear the brunt of the blowback. Several studies attest to the significant role Saudi nationals have played in the conflict. Of the 154 Arab fighters killed in Iraq between September

2004 and March 2005, 61 percent were from Saudi Arabia. Another report concluded that of the 235 suicide bombers named on Web sites since mid-2004 as having perpetrated attacks in Iraq, more than 50 percent were Saudi nationals. Today, the Saudi government is exporting its jihadist problem instead of dealing with it, just as the Egyptians did during the Afghan war.

A SWITCH IN TIME

American success in Iraq would deny today's jihadists the symbolic victory that they seek. But with that outcome so uncertain, U.S. policymakers must focus on dealing with the jihadists in Iraq now— by limiting the numbers entering the fight and breaking the mechanism that would otherwise generate blowback after the war.

The foreign jihadists in Iraq need to be separated from the local insurgents through the political process. Success in that mission will require Iraq's Sunni Arabs to remain consistently engaged in the political process. Shiite and Kurdish leaders will have to back down from their efforts to create semiautonomous states in the north and the south. But the prospects for these developments appear dim at the moment, and reaching a durable agreement may increasingly be beyond U.S. influence.

To raise the odds of success, the United States must deliver more security to central Iraq. This means securing Iraq's borders, especially with Syria, to block the flow of foreign fighters into the country. The repeated U.S. military operations in western Iraq since May have shown that at present there are insufficient forces to disrupt insurgent supply lines running along the Euphrates River to the Syrian border. Accomplishing this objective would require either more U.S. troops or a much larger force of well-trained Iraqi troops. For the moment, neither of those options seems viable, and so additional U.S. soldiers should be rotated out of Iraq's cities and into the western deserts and border towns, transitioning the control of certain urban areas to the Iraqi military and police.

Foreign governments must also silence calls to jihad and deny radicals sanctuary once this war ends. After the Soviet defeat, jihadists too often found refuge in places as varied as Brooklyn and Khartoum, where radical clerics offered religious justifications for continuing jihad. To date, some governments have not taken the necessary steps to clamp down on the new generation of jihadists. Although the Saudis largely silenced their radical clerics following the terrorist attacks in Riyadh in May 2003, 26 clerics were still permitted late in 2004 to call for jihad against U.S. troops in Iraq. The United States must press the Saudi government to end these appeals and restrict its nationals from entering

Iraq. In the long run, measures against radical preaching are in Riyadh's best interest, too, since the blowback from Iraq is likely to be as painful for Saudi Arabia as the blowback from Afghanistan was for Egypt and Algeria during the 1990s.

Finally, the U.S. intelligence community, in conjunction with foreign intelligence services, should work on creating a database that identifies and tracks foreign fighters, their known associates, and their spiritual mentors. If such a database had been created during the Afghan war, the United States would have been far better prepared for al Qaeda's subsequent terror campaign.

President Jimmy Carter's national security adviser, Zbigniew Brzezinski, once asked of the Soviet defeat in Afghanistan: "What is most important to the history of the world? The Taliban or the collapse of the Soviet empire? Some stirred-up Muslims or the liberation of Central Europe and the end of the Cold War?" Today, the Bush administration is implicitly arguing a similar point: that the establishment of a democratic Iraqi state is a project of overriding importance for the United States and the world, which in due course will eclipse memories of the insurgency. But such a viewpoint minimizes the fact that the war in Iraq is already breeding a new generation of terrorists. The lesson of the decade of terror that followed the Afghan war was that underestimating the importance of blowback has severe consequences. Repeating the mistake in regard to Iraq could lead to even deadlier outcomes.

Reprinted by permission of FOREIGN AFFAIRS, (November/December 2005). Copyright 2007 by the Council on Foreign Relations, Inc.

Geographically speaking, terrorists can come from just about anywhere. Iraq and Afghanistan, as the preceding essay showed, excel at turning out experienced cadres. But where do the trainees come from in the first place? Where are perfectly normal young people radicalized and prepared for a life of violence? If the recruits are Muslims, attention immediately turns to the Middle East and South Asia. According to popular opinion, millions of young Muslims stand prepared to fill any vacancy that might open in the global terrorist ranks. Often poor and disaffected, these men (and increasingly, women) have grown up in a region polarized by decades of bloody warfare and sectarian conflict. They have been raised on a steady diet of hate, or so it is thought. Brutality has become a commonplace occurrence for many. All of this has been amplified by educations gained in the region's madrasahs, religious schools that have a reputation for encouraging religious intolerance and preaching holy war.

The validity of this reputation has rarely been challenged. Time and again, otherwise informed and thoughtful commentators have identified madrasahs as wellsprings of violence and the ideological source of the world's Islamic militants.

The next author, Alexander Evans, refutes this claim. Evans acknowledges the fact that some madrasahs are, in fact, little more than hate mills that churn out fanatics. But overwhelmingly, he contends, madrasahs and other Muslim schools represent a stabilizing influence in parts of the world that are in desperate need of alternatives to the rough education of the street and back alley. When attempting to locate the points of origin for violent extremists, madrasahs might not be the places to start. They are not all terrorist nurseries, Evans argues persuasively. Rather than pushing to close or tightly regulate madrasahs, he asks the West to look again at Islamic education and try to understand it.

Understanding Madrasahs: How Threatening Are They?
Alexander Evans

Madrasahs, the religious schools that educate millions of students in the Muslim world, have been blamed for all sorts of ills since the attacks of September 11, 2001. Critics have denounced them as dens of terror, hatcheries for suicide bombers, and repositories of medievalism. As Samina Ahmed and Andrew Stroehlein of the International Crisis Group wrote in *The Washington Post* after last July's London bombings, "Jihadi extremism is still propagated at radical madrassas in Pakistan. ... And now, it seems, the hatred these madrassas breed is spilling blood in Western cities as well."

These criticisms have focused on the few dozen Pakistani madrasahs that served as de facto training grounds for jihadists fighting the Soviet occupation of Afghanistan in the 1980s. Many of these jihadists went on to become foot soldiers in later campaigns, including those against Indian rule over Kashmir and against Shiite Muslims within Pakistan. They also helped forge the Taliban and gave succor and support to Osama bin Laden. From this record, critics have put together a seemingly convincing charge sheet against madrasahs across the Muslim world. They extrapolate from this relatively small number of problem madrasahs in Pakistan and conclude that all madrasahs breed fanatics.

But they are wrong. The majority of madrasahs actually present an opportunity, not a threat. For young village kids, it may be their only path to literacy. For many orphans and the rural poor, madrasahs provide essential social services: education and lodging for children who otherwise could well find themselves the victims of forced labor, sex trafficking, or other abuse. And for U.S. and European policymakers, madrasahs offer an important arena for public diplomacy—a chance to ensure that the Muslim leaders of tomorrow do not see the West as an enemy inherently hostile to all Muslim institutions.

Rather than undermining the madrasah system, then, Western policymakers should engage it. Beards and bombast may make for good newspaper copy, but the reality of the madrasah system is far different: it is characterized by both orthodoxy and diversity and is host to a quiet debate about reform. It is in the interest of the West to ensure that the outliers—truly extremist madrasahs—are contained and advocates or apologists for terrorism duly prosecuted. But it is equally important for policy-makers to pursue this goal carefully, by encouraging internal debate rather than demanding changes from above. The best incentive for reform is competition rather than control.

TENURED RADICALS?

The Western consensus on madrasahs assumes that some of them produce terrorists and many others contribute to radicalization in less direct ways. But the evidence of a direct link to terrorism remains weak. Indeed, according to Marc Sageman's recent study *Understanding Terror Networks*, two-thirds of contemporary al Qaeda–affiliated terrorists went to state or Western-style colleges. Like the terrorist Ahmed Sheikh (who was a contemporary of mine at the London School of Economics), terrorists today are more likely to have gone through the regular educational system. Many are newly religious rebels rather than regular *ulama* (clergy), created by modernity rather than by a madrasah.

In fact, despite the hype and the headlines, remarkably little serious work has been done on the subject of madrasahs. (This problem, fortunately, is slowly changing, with academics such as Saleem Ali, Tahir Andrabi, and Yoginder Sikand paving the way with detailed, evidence-based studies.) Few journalists bother to get to know more than a token institution, and most academics shy away from studying them; the leaders of madrasahs themselves prefer to get on with what they do rather than talk about it. There are tens of thousands of madrasahs, with millions of students, but the numerical data on them—usually drawn from government statistics, media speculation, or the dubious assertions of madrasah defenders and denouncers—are generally unreliable. In India, for example, estimates of the number of madrasahs range from 3,000 to 30,000, with up to 1.5 million students estimated to be enrolled. Some reports claim that Bangladesh has 64,000 madrasahs. Pakistan, meanwhile, is said to have anywhere from 400,000 to 1.7 million students enrolled.

Madrasahs serve parts of developing countries that governments never reach. Turn off any main highway in Pakistan, Bangladesh, or northern India, drive 15 miles down a poor-quality road, and more often than not you will find a small madrasah, funded by donations and occasionally fees, in the nearest village. Even in the cities, where there are many more government and other private schools, madrasahs survive as providers of social services for Muslim orphans (many of whom are taken in and brought up there for free). Meanwhile, many Muslim parents choose to send their sons (it is usually sons) to madrasahs because they consider the education they get there to be a respectable one.

The madrasah system is a thousand years old. It originated in eleventh-century Baghdad, and the earliest recorded South Asian madrasah was established in Ajmer (now a city in India) in 1191. In medieval times, madrasahs were instruments of the state—funded by rulers and steadfastly loyal—and focused on Islamic jurisprudence (*fiqh*). Over time, with the advent of the Mughal empire in South Asia, this curriculum expanded, first to include philosophy, logic, and the rational disciplines (*maqalat*) and then to include the study of reports of the words and deeds of the Prophet Muhammad (*hadith*) as well. Madrasahs were also bastions of social exclusion. They served as prestigious training schools for imperial officials and religious scholars, catering to and funded by the Muslim elite.

The advent of British control over South Asia, however, undermined this elite and led to important changes in the madrasah system. English replaced Persian as the language of official correspondence in the 1830s (thanks to the East India Company), and missionaries began establishing English-language alternatives to religious schools. The biggest change came in the aftermath of the failed 1857 uprising against British rule in India. Muslim scholars, already sidelined, retreated into traditional education—seeking to defend Islam against the onslaught of Christian influence, even as they watched the death of Mughal rule in India.

From this transition, the Darul Uloom madrasah emerged in Deoband, India. Established entirely with private support in 1865, it became the center for a newfound scriptural conservatism in Islam. The foundation of Darul Uloom also marked a closing of doors to modern knowledge, which was now seen as polluting because of its association with the British. Deobandis (as those associated with Darul Uloom became known) worked hard to spread their message across northern India, and the social composition of madrasahs began to change, becoming less affluent and more rural.

Darul Uloom, where 10,000 young men compete for 800 spots in any given year, remains the center of the Deobandi movement. The movement is still ultraconservative, and it helped define the Taliban's purist ideology.

In large part because of its role in shaping the Taliban's rule, the Deobandi movement is the prism through which most observers analyze the entire madrasah system. But there are other influential schools, and many of them are less conservative. The thousands of Barelvi madrasahs across South Asia, including Pakistan, take a broader view of heterodox Sufi traditions. Shiite madrasahs are primarily designed for elementary education and leave higher study to learning centers in the Middle East. Since the 1940s, the Islamist Jamaat-e-Islami—an avowedly modern Muslim organization dedicated to combining a conservative, Islamist worldview with a commitment to education across the modern sciences—has established many schools of its own, although formally it does not support madrasahs.

To be sure, madrasahs are naturally narrow-minded institutions. Non-Muslims, particularly Jews, are regularly portrayed in a negative or hostile light and described as *najis* (impure) or *jahil* (ignorant). But it is wrong to blame madrasahs alone for such views: the same prejudice is prevalent in bazaars, private homes, and even government-funded schools in the Muslim world.

Critics have also focused on the sources of funding for madrasahs—which are not tax dollars but charity and, in some cases, tuition fees. Some of the charitable funding comes from overseas, especially from radical Islamists in the Gulf region (although these funds have decreased of late). The largest madrasahs receive over $1.5 million a year, but many smaller ones exist on a few hundred dollars a year, more of which comes from local funding than is usually assumed. In any case, funds from extremists have only a limited influence on individual madrasahs. Even after five decades of funding from radical Islamists in the Persian Gulf, many South Asian madrasahs are still run by teachers who reject Wahabbism and its various sisters. In fact, across South Asia, extremists—as distinct from ultra-conservatives—actually control only a tiny portion of the madrasahs.

It is also wrong to assume, as most current commentary does, that madrasahs have stood still for the past several centuries. Although there could certainly be much more, there is plenty of innovation within the world of madrasahs. In my visits to dozens of institutions in Bangladesh, India, and Pakistan, I have found English classes, a journalism-training school, an electrician-training center, and computer labs. I have met stimulating and thoughtful principals who are determined to provide the best possible education. I have also sat down with dour and insipid madrasah directors suspicious of anything that might diminish their standing in their school or the wider community. And once or twice, I have bumped into seriously nasty radicals. (Unsurprisingly, a great deal depends on the individual running a madrasah.)

Even Darul Uloom is slowly evolving. Over the past five years, it has introduced English and computing. Some 40 pupils— just over one percent of the student body— learn English. Within the Deobandi movement, there is a growing debate about madrasah reform. So far, the conservatives have dominated. But senior *ulama* now welcome greater contact with the outside world. "We should not be shy of media people," one told me when I visited in July 2005. "We are not thieves."

NO MADRASAH IS AN ISLAND

For hundreds of years, madrasahs have changed as Muslim societies have changed. The change has always been a mixture of resisting, reacting, and innovating—just as with educational systems anywhere.

The past decade has produced fresh incentives for reform—and madrasahs are slowly responding. First, there has been a sharp rise in English-language private schools, since middle-class parents want their children to have the right skills to get good jobs. The most prestigious madrasahs, such as Darul Uloom, dismiss this trend as irrelevant because it has not led to a fall in applications. But in smaller towns, the rise of private schools has already limited the ability of fee-charging madrasahs to attract enough students. In some cases, this problem has stimulated broader thinking about including English-language instruction.

Innovation and reform also stem from a recognition that madrasah graduates are more likely to access decent tertiary education and a wider range of employment opportunities if the curriculum is widened. In India, some madrasah students are already breaking through—becoming doctors, lawyers, and software engineers. They often find that the discipline of madrasah training helps them focus on further studies, even if the educational base they began with was narrower (but deeper) than that of many of their peers. And madrasah students themselves are keen to see reform, including the introduction of English or local languages such as Hindi or Bengali alongside the traditional Islamic subjects.

Cynics rightly point out that reform is also being stimulated by the emphasis on missionary activity (*dawa*). Leading *ulama* are recognizing that in order to reach non-Muslims (and many Muslims besides), English is an increasingly important medium. And in order to counter other religions, more than a basic (and polemical) grounding is needed in Christianity, Hinduism, and Buddhism. These leaders are eager to ensure that the next generation of Muslim *ulama* can communicate in English. Generational change is also playing its part. Some of the younger innovators share a commitment to Islamic education but also want to attract bright and able students.

Given all the media attacks on madrasahs, a backlash would not be surprising. Instead, *ulama* within the madrasah system are increasingly open to communication with the outside world. In India, leading lights of the madrasah movement have since 1995 been regularly calling for greater interaction with the media, intellectuals, and government officials. And most important, no madrasah is an island. Deobandi *ulama* may have issued a fatwa against television, but cellular phones are ubiquitous in most madrasahs. Madrasah students do not live lives of seclusion, despite the intensity of the curriculum.

SENSE AND SENSITIVITY

Governments have adopted two basic approaches to madrasahs: regulation and reform. The first approach involves extending or introducing government regulations, ranging from compulsory madrasahregistration schemes to curriculum reform to Pakistani President Pervez Musharraf's July 2005 ruling that all foreign students must leave Pakistani madrasahs. Governments have also demanded that independent madrasahs adopt the country's regular core curriculum. Other steps have included registering students, creating an approved register of principals, imposing financial controls—or shutting down particular problem madrasahs. Reform interventions, meanwhile, seek to undercut madrasahs by improving state capacity. This usually means spending large sums of money to extend government schools into areas they previously did not reach or making state education compulsory.

Both strategies can run into the sand. The trouble with regulatory interventions is they can easily prove excessive or even counterproductive. Registration is not unreasonable, but it has little effect other than to create lists of institutions, students, and principals. Enforced curriculum reform is likely to generate a backlash. Madrasahs as a whole are designed to transmit a religious tradition, and their independence is a core part of their identity. Many graduates from the better madrasahs resent any notion of enforced regulation, and these same graduates are often the best critics of the madrasah system, recognizing its shortfalls as they go on either to run madrasahs of their own or to enter mainstream employment.

Given the scale of the challenge, reform interventions are also bound to fail. Spending more money—whether government or donor funds—on education in general is not going to displace madrasahs anytime soon. Improving the reach and effectiveness of public education will take a long time, and parents often choose madrasahs for their children even when state-provided education is available—often for the prestige of having a son study Islam and enter an Islamic profession.

When it comes to the choice between forcing change and fostering change, India, with a Muslim population of 138 million or more, illustrates one way forward. Historically, madrasahs there have had a lot of independence, and Article 30(1) of the Indian constitution guarantees minorities (Muslims, Sikhs, and Christians) the right to establish and administer their own educational institutions. But the Indian government still has recourse if any one madrasah becomes problematic: it can invoke laws against incitement to violence if a madrasah principal advocates terrorism.

Indian educational officials have occasionally considered a more hard-line approach, especially in the late 1990s, when concerns about radicalization were abnormally high. But after careful consideration, the same officials have come to the conclusion that the best change comes from within: let madrasah speak to madrasah, and principal to principal, so that the reformers can influence the others. One initiative that has come out of this approach is a scheme to pay for English, math, and science teachers in private madrasahs that choose to participate. If a madrasah principal decides to apply, he gets a fully funded teacher in one of these subjects. It makes good sense for the madrasah (since it gets a free resource) and good sense for the government, too, as it thereby demonstrates the benefits of having this subject in addition to the traditional curriculum. In 2001, 3,500 out of 6,000 madrasahs in the Indian state of Madhya Pradesh received funds for teachers of modern subjects, reaching some 175,000 students. The Indian government has also provided teacher training for madrasah teachers in Delhi.

The Indian approach is predicated on consent. It is both sensitive and sensible. India's leaders are aware of the dangers of a backlash if they intervene forcefully. And unlike the thinking underlying much of the overblown press commentary, the basic assumption behind the government's approach is that madrasahs play a valuable role in society, even if the education they provide is more narrow than it should be.

THE INDIVISIBLE HAND

Madrasahs do not need to be closed, contained, or cut down to size. Thousands play an important social role. And the leaders of most madrasahs are willing to consider changing the way they work, although they are bound to defend what they stand for.

To be sure, there are problem madrasahs, led by extremists who preach venom. These madrasahs, many of which are in Pakistan, tend to trigger provocative media coverage. But they do not dominate. Go to the largest neighboring madrasah of a "problem" madrasah, and you will usually find a group of tut-tutting *ulama* saying, gently but insistently, that their madrasah "isn't political like that one." Problem madrasahs need to be challenged, but as individual institutions, each with its own problems that do not necessarily reflect the reality of the entire system. The particular fault often lies with the principal, rather than with the madrasah as a whole. And most countries have the legislation in place to proceed against these principals if they incite violence or coach potential terrorists. Passing new rules or restrictions makes little sense if the existing laws are not being applied effectively.

Of course, the most effective challenge to these problem madrasahs will come from their peers, not state intervention. Al Qaeda is as much an idea as it is a movement or an organization, and ideas, good and bad, often work like infections. Distant regulators, disgusted officials, and worried Westerners can only do so much, but madrasah principals, graduates, and *ulama* wield enormous power. In short, the best debate on madrasah reform will come from within.

What is needed most is a thoughtful, evidence-based approach to madrasahs. Policymakers should visit them, research them, and understand them, all the while being sure to understand that their actions could have unintended consequences. They should encourage modernization but avoid insisting on secularization, which would be taken as a declaration of war on Muslim education. They should seek to stimulate conversation and competition among madrasahs while allowing them their freedom. Attempting to change madrasahs through compulsion and control is unlikely to deliver positive results. Reform of the madrasah system will ultimately be spurred by competition from within—and the more competition, the better.

Reprinted by permission of FOREIGN AFFAIRS, (January/February 2006). Copyright 2007 by the Council on Foreign Relations, Inc.

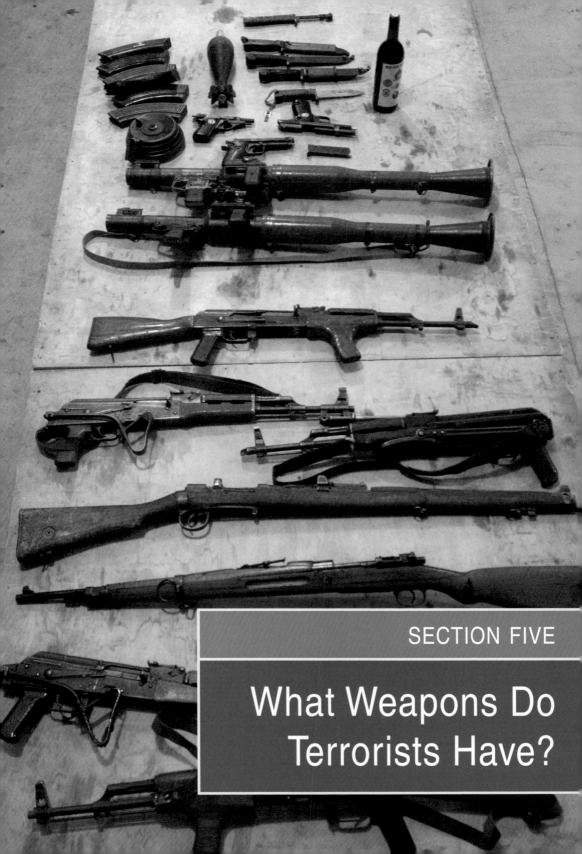

What Weapons Do
Terrorists Have?

Piracy is often dismissed as quaint, an antique practice belonging to a bygone era. Mention the word "pirate," and one is likely to conjure up images of peg-legged buccaneers sailing the Caribbean under a Jolly Roger flag. Few people would think of pirates as well-trained terrorists employing the latest technology and prowling the seas in high-speed attack boats. That is, however, the profile of the modern pirate. As one writer on the subject put it, "the scourge of the seventeenth and eighteenth centuries . . . has returned with deadly and terrifying results."*

Savage as they could be, the pirates of yesteryear posed nowhere near the threat presented by today's seafaring terrorists. Using state-of-the-art equipment and exhibiting sophisticated skills, terrorists have gone to sea, potentially jeopardizing global trade and putting at risk any nation with significant port operations. The U.S. Coast Guard and the FBI both recognize an imminent danger of pirate attacks and have concluded that "cruise ships, ferries, and container ships are likely targets for terrorists using a bomb or a small boat packed with explosives or by taking hostages."** The open seas are no longer beyond the reach of violent extremists.

Gal Luft and Anne Korin outline this troubling new form of terror in the following essay. They argue that governments can expect economic chaos or worse if they make the mistake of minimizing the danger of piracy in the post–September 11 world. Global terrorists have already struck airports and public transportation systems, resulting in great losses of life and disruption of economic activity. After the 2001 attacks in New York City and the later train and subway bombings in Madrid and London, elaborate precautions were taken in order to prevent recurrences. Ports, shipping facilities, and ocean-going vessels, however, have not been given the same level of attention. If the next essay is correct, this is an error that invites disaster.

NOTES

* John S. Burnett, *Dangerous Waters: Modern Piracy and Terror on the High Seas* (New York: Dutton, 2002), 9.
** Eric Lipton, "Report Sees Confusion Likely In a Sea Attack by Terrorists," *New York Times*, April 4, 2006, A17.

Terrorism Goes to Sea
GAL LUFT AND ANNE KORIN

A NEW NEXUS

Since the attacks of September 11, 2001, security experts have frequently invoked a 200-year-old model to guide leaders contending with the threat of Islamist terrorism: the war on piracy. In the first years of the nineteenth century, Mediterranean pirates, with the support of the Barbary states of northern Africa, would capture merchant ships and hold their crews for ransom. In response, the United States launched the Barbary wars, the first successful effort by the young republic to protect its citizens from a ruthless, unconventional enemy by fighting a protracted struggle overseas.

Such experts, however, fail to realize that the popular perception that the international community has eliminated sea piracy is far from true. Not only has piracy never been eradicated, but the number of pirate attacks on ships has also tripled in the past decade—putting piracy at its highest level in modern history. And contrary to the stereotype, today's pirates are often trained fighters aboard speedboats equipped with satellite phones and global positioning systems and armed with automatic weapons, antitank missiles, and grenades.

Most disturbingly, the scourges of piracy and terrorism are increasingly intertwined: piracy on the high seas is becoming a key tactic of terrorist groups. Unlike the pirates of old, whose sole objective was quick commercial gain, many of today's pirates are maritime terrorists with an ideological bent and a broad political agenda. This nexus of piracy and terrorism is especially dangerous for energy markets: most of the world's oil and gas is shipped through the world's most piracy-infested waters.

ROUGH WATERS

Water covers almost three-quarters of the globe and is home to roughly 50,000 large ships, which carry 80 percent of the world's traded cargo. The sea has always been an anarchic domain. Unlike land and air, it is barely policed, even today. Since many shipping companies do not report incidents of piracy, for fear of raising their insurance premiums and prompting protracted, time-consuming investigations, the precise extent of piracy is unknown. But statistics from the International Maritime

Bureau (IMB), a piracy watchdog, suggest that both the frequency and the violence of acts of piracy have increased in recent years. In 2003, ship owners reported 445 attacks, in which 92 seafarers were killed or reported missing and 359 were assaulted and taken hostage. (Ships were hijacked in 19 of these cases and boarded in 311.) From 2002 to 2003, the number of those killed and taken hostage in attacks nearly doubled. Pirates have also increased their tactical sophistication, often surrounding a target ship with several boats and firing machine guns and antitank missiles to force it to stop. As Singapore's Deputy Prime Minister Tony Tan recently warned, "piracy is entering a new phase; recent attacks have been conducted with almost military precision. The perpetrators are well-trained, have well laid out plans." The total damage caused by piracy—due to losses of ships and cargo and to rising insurance costs—now amounts to $16 billion per year.

Many pirates, especially those in eastern Asia, belong to organized crime syndicates comprising corrupt officials, port workers, hired thugs, and businessmen who dispose of the booty. Grossly underpaid maritime security personnel have also begun to enter the business; many are complicit, and some are actively involved, in attacks.

Pirates and Islamist terrorist groups have long operated in the same areas, including the Arabian Sea, the South China Sea, and in waters off the coast of western Africa. Now, in the face of massive international efforts to freeze their finances, terrorist groups have come to view piracy as a potentially rich source of funding. This appeal is particularly apparent in the Strait of Malacca, the 500-mile corridor separating Indonesia and Malaysia, where 42 percent of pirate attacks took place in 2003. According to Indonesia's state intelligence agency, detained senior members of Jemaah Islamiyah, the al Qaeda–linked Indonesian terrorist group, have admitted that the group has considered launching attacks on Malacca shipping. And uniformed members of the Free Aceh Movement, an Indonesian separatist group that is also one of the most radical Islamist movements in the world, have been hijacking vessels and taking their crews hostage at an increasing rate. The protracted ransom negotiations yield considerable sums—the going rate is approximately $100,000 per ship—later used to procure weapons for sustained operations against the Indonesian government. In some cases, the Free Aceh Movement has demanded the release of members detained by the government in exchange for hostages.

The string of maritime attacks perpetrated in recent years demonstrates that terror has indeed gone to sea. In January 2000, al Qaeda attempted to ram a boat loaded with explosives into the USS *The Sullivans* in Yemen. (The attack failed only because the boat sank under the weight of its lethal payload.) After this initial failure, al Qaeda suicide bombers in a speedboat packed with explosives blew a hole in the USS *Cole*, killing 17 sailors, in October 2000. In October 2002, an explosives-laden boat hit the French oil tanker *Limburg* off the coast of Yemen. In February 2004, the southern Philippines–based Abu Sayyaf claimed responsibility for an explosion on a large ferry that killed at least 100 people. And according to FBI Director Robert Mueller, "any number of attacks on ships have been thwarted." In June 2002, for example, the Moroccan government arrested a group of al Qaeda operatives suspected of plotting raids on British and U.S. tankers passing through the Strait of Gibraltar.

Terrorist groups such as Hezbollah, Jemaah Islamiyah, the Popular Front for the Liberation of Palestine–General Command, and Sri Lanka's Tamil Tigers have long sought to develop a maritime capability. Intelligence agencies estimate that al Qaeda and its affiliates now own dozens of phantom ships—hijacked vessels that have been repainted and renamed and operate under false documentation, manned by crews with fake passports and forged competency certificates. Security experts have long warned that terrorists might try to ram a ship loaded with explosive cargo, perhaps even a weapon of mass destruction, into a major port or terminal. Such an attack could bring international trade to a halt, inflicting multi-billion-dollar damage on the world economy.

BLACK GOLD

Following the attack on the *Limburg*, Osama bin Laden released an audio tape warning of attacks on economic targets in the West: "By God, the youths of God are preparing for you things that would fill your hearts with terror and target your economic lifeline until you stop your oppression and aggression." It is no secret that one of the most effective ways for terrorists to disrupt the global economy is to attack oil supplies—in the words of al Qaeda spokesmen, "the provision line and the feeding artery of the life of the crusader nation."

With global oil consumption at 80 million barrels per day and spare production capacity gradually eroding, the oil market has little wiggle room. As a result, supply disruptions can have a devastating impact on oil prices—as terrorists well know. U.S. Energy Secretary Spencer Abraham has repeatedly warned that "terrorists are looking for opportunities to impact the world economy" by targeting energy infrastructure. In recent years, terrorists have targeted pipelines, refineries, pumping stations, and tankers in some of the world's most important energy reservoirs, including Iraq, Nigeria, Saudi Arabia, and Yemen.

In fact, since September 11, 2001, strikes on oil targets have become almost routine. In October 2001, Tamil Tiger separatists carried out a coordinated suicide attack by five boats on an oil tanker off northern Sri Lanka. Oil facilities in Nigeria, the United States' fifth-largest oil supplier, have under-gone numerous attacks. In Colombia, leftist rebels have blown so many holes in the 480-mile Caño Limón–Coveñas pipeline that it has become known as "the flute." And in Iraq, more than 150 attacks on the country's 4,000-mile pipeline system have hindered the effort to resume oil production, denying Iraqis funds necessary for the reconstruction effort. In April 2004, suicide bombers in three boats blew themselves up in and around the Basra terminal zone, one of the most heavily guarded facilities of its kind in the world.

Particularly vulnerable to oil terrorism is Saudi Arabia, which holds a quarter of the globe's oil reserves and, as the world's leading exporter, accounts for one-tenth of daily oil production. Al Qaeda is well aware that a successful attack on one of the kingdom's major oil facilities would rattle the world and send oil prices through the ceiling. In the summer of 2002, a group of Saudis was arrested for plotting to sabotage the world's largest offshore oil-loading facility, Ras Tanura, through which up to a third of Saudi oil flows. More recently, in May 2004, jihadist gunmen opened fire on foreign workers in Yanbu, Saudi Arabia's petrochemical complex on the Red Sea, killing five foreign nationals. Later in the same month, Islamic extremists seized and killed 22 foreign oil workers in the Saudi city of Khobar. All of these attacks caused major disruptions in the oil market and a spike in insurance premiums, bringing oil prices to their highest level since 1990.

Whereas land targets are relatively well protected, the super-extended energy umbilical cord that extends by sea to connect the West and the Asian economies with the Middle East is more vulnerable than ever. Sixty percent of the world's oil is shipped by approximately 4,000 slow and cumbersome tankers. These vessels have little protection, and when attacked, they have nowhere to hide. (Except on Russian and Israeli ships, the only weapons crewmembers have today to ward off attackers are high-powered fire hoses and spotlights.)

If a single tanker were attacked on the high seas, the impact on the energy market would be marginal. But geography forces the tankers to pass through strategic chokepoints, many of which are located in areas where terrorists with maritime capabilities are active. These channels—major points of vulnerability for the world economy—are so narrow at points that a single burning supertanker and its spreading oil slick could block the route for other vessels. Were terrorist pirates to hijack a large bulk carrier or oil tanker, sail it into one of the chokepoints, and scuttle

Asia, but also allow shippers to bypass the Strait of Malacca. In the same vein, to reduce pressure on the Strait of Hormuz, the oil pipeline that traverses Israel could be expanded. Russian oil from the Black Sea enters the pipeline at the Israeli port of Ashqelon on the Mediterranean coast and flows to Elat on the Red Sea, where it is loaded onto tankers and shipped to Asia. This route provides a much shorter link between the Mediterranean and Asia.

Most important, as the world's energy supply is likely to remain a terrorist target, the risk must be reduced not only by improving the security of ocean thruways, but also by looking inward: by replacing imported energy with next-generation energy derived from domestic energy resources. Such a shift would increase energy independence for the free world and minimize the need to transport oil across the globe—thus reducing the world's vulnerability to a catastrophic disruption of its energy supply by terrorists at sea.

Reprinted by permission of FOREIGN AFFAIRS, (November/December 2004). Copyright 2007 by the Council on Foreign Relations, Inc.

Chemical and biological weapons touch perhaps the deepest chords of human fear. The mere thought of their use evokes images of hideous lingering death on a massive scale. Poisons and pathogens are silent killers whose victims suffer gruesome and painful ends. It is no great surprise that even the remote possibility of such weapons falling into the hands of terrorists is enough to generate widespread public anxiety. Nor is such unease entirely misplaced. Even before the recent small-scale biological and chemical attacks noted in the next essay, the world caught a glimpse during World War I of the kinds of casualties that result from the use of toxic agents. Photographs of soldiers blinded or burned by gas and images of the bloated bodies of troops who put on their protective masks too slowly horrified anyone who saw them.

Pictures of human beings maimed or killed by chemical bombs are etched into the popular consciousness. History will forever recall the terrible suffering and death caused by the Japanese use of biological weapons in China during World War II. People justly fear the effects of pathogens such as the one also used by Japan to cause an outbreak of bubonic plague in the Chinese countryside. What would happen, many ask, if terrorists acquired and used nerve agents, anthrax, or botulinum as a weapon? The idea that the public water supply could be secretly tainted, the food supply quietly contaminated, or the air made toxic by some exotic gas is exquisitely terrifying.

The actual danger posed by chemical and biological weapons, however, might not equal the deadliness of its imaginary counterpart. In other words, an exaggerated fear of their use might be more damaging than the actual employment of gas or bacteria, given the difficulties associated with their manufacture and application in the context of a terrorist strike. This is what Jonathan B. Tucker argued in April 2000. Tucker, while not ignoring the very real possibility that terrorists might add chemical and biological weapons to their arsenal, urged his readers to remember how many obstacles would have to be overcome before they could cause the sort of mass destruction that has become the terrorist trademark.

Chemical and Biological Terrorism: How Real a Threat?
JONATHAN B. TUCKER

The Clinton administration contends that terrorists armed with chemical and biological weapons pose a new strategic threat to the United States. In January 1999, President Bill Clinton said it was "highly likely" that a terrorist group would launch or threaten a chemical or biological attack against a civilian target within the next few years, and that this possibility kept him "awake at night." Defense Secretary William Cohen warned in July 1999 that "a plague more monstrous than anything we have experienced could spread with all the irrevocability of ink on tissue paper." And in October, ABC's "Nightline" aired a weeklong docudrama in which a hypothetical attack with anthrax bacteria on the subway system of a major American city results in more than 50,000 deaths.

This drumbeat of frightening official pronouncements and sensational media reports has helped to build political support in Congress for a major increase in spending on programs to counter the threat of chemical and biological terrorism—up to $1.4 billion in the fiscal year 2000 budget. Yet how likely is the threat that terrorists will resort to toxic weapons? Government concerns about chemical and biological terrorism have been driven largely by the vulnerability of large urban centers and the growing availability of knowledge and production equipment that have peaceful applications but could be turned to military ends. Such considerations alone, however, do not provide a solid basis for decision making about the measures needed to meet the terrorism challenge. Only a realistic threat assessment based on an analysis of terrorist motivations, patterns of behavior, and likely targets will make it possible to develop tailored and cost-effective strategies for prevention and response.

TOXIC AGENTS AS TERRORIST WEAPONS

Despite all the hype, it would be wrong to conclude that the threat of chemical or biological terrorism is merely a figment of President Clinton's imagination. The current wave of official concern began in March 1995, when members of the Japanese religious cult Aum Shinrikyo released the nerve agent sarin in the Tokyo subway, killing 12 people and injuring more than a thousand. Although many analysts feared that this attack by Aum Shinrikyo (which recently changed its name to Aleph, the first letter of the Hebrew alphabet) was the harbinger of a new and more deadly form of terrorism, five years have passed and a copycat attack has yet to materialize.

The Aum Shinrikyo incident did demonstrate that at least some terrorists are motivated to acquire and use chemical or biological agents, and that the shock value of an attack could capture media attention and deeply frighten the general public. Nevertheless, the common tendency to classify chemical and biological agents as weapons of mass destruction is highly misleading. In fact, the ability of these materials to inflict mass casualties is not an inherent property but is highly dependent on the type and quantity of agent released and the means of delivery.

Chemical warfare agents are synthetic, super-toxic poisons that are inhaled or absorbed through the skin. Odorless, tasteless, and invisible, nerve agents such as sarin cause seizures and loss of voluntary control, and can kill in minutes by respiratory paralysis. Persistent nerve agents, such as VX, can contaminate buildings and people, sowing disruption and chaos in the affected area. Yet chemical weapons have major drawbacks for terrorist use. Large quantities of nerve agent—about a metric ton of sarin per square kilometer—must be dispersed to inflict mass casualties. Dispersal is difficult in open areas and thus unpredictable in its effects, and nerve agents can be countered with timely medical intervention such as the administration of antidotes.

Biological warfare agents are microbes that cause illness or death in people, livestock, or crops; this category also includes naturally occurring poisons such as botulinum toxin (produced by a bacterium) and ricin (extracted from the seeds of the castor bean plant). Most microbial agents developed for biological warfare, such as the bacteria that cause anthrax and tularemia, are infectious but not contagious. Because only people directly exposed to the agent would become sick, the effects of a terrorist attack would be self-limiting. Two exceptions are plague bacteria and smallpox virus, both of which are contagious and could spawn serious epidemics. But plague bacteria are fragile and difficult to weaponize, and the smallpox virus was eradicated from nature in 1977 by a global vaccination campaign and now exists officially in only two laboratories, making it difficult for terrorists to acquire.

Because microbial pathogens are living and reproduce inside the host to cause disease, they are theoretically far more potent than chemical weapons per unit weight: inflicting a 50 percent fatality rate over a square kilometer would require about a metric ton of sarin, but only a few kilograms of anthrax spores. Nevertheless, to be effective, anthrax spores would have to be dispersed as an aerosol cloud of microscopic particles small enough to be inhaled and retained in the lungs. The casualty-producing effects of a bioterrorist attack would therefore depend on several factors, including the type of agent used, the delivery system, the quantity of agent dispersed, the physical form of the agent (for example, wet slurry or dry powder), the efficiency of aerosolization, and the prevailing atmospheric and weather conditions at the time of release.

Biological weapons also have operational liabilities. Whereas chemical nerve agents such as sarin act in minutes, microbial pathogens induce illness only after an incubation period of up to several days, and their effects can vary depending on the immunological competence of the host. Because of the delay between infection and disease, an outbreak resulting from an act of bioterrorism might not be recognized for weeks, diluting its impact as an instrument of terror or coercion.

ASSESSING THE THREAT

In an effort to assess the threat of toxic terrorism, the Monterey Institute's Center for Nonproliferation Studies in Monterey, California, has compiled a worldwide database of documented incidents involving the terrorist use of chemical or biological agents from 1900 to the end of 1999, as well as a much larger collection of criminally motivated incidents, unsuccessful plots, and hoaxes. The Monterey database contains 101 cases of terrorist use, two-thirds of which took place outside the United States. Altogether, they produced a total of 103 fatalities and 5,554 injuries.

What does this historical record tell us about the most likely patterns of chemical and biological terrorism? Contrary to conventional wisdom, the documented attacks in which these weapons were used were small in scale and generally produced fewer casualties than conventional explosives. The sole United States fatality occurred in 1973, when the Symbionese Liberation Army used cyanide-tainted bullets to assassinate Marcus Foster, the Oakland, California, school superintendent. (Since the victim was shot eight times with a .38-caliber handgun, he would have died in any case.) In another incident in 1984, members of the Oregon-based Rajneeshee cult contaminated restaurant salad bars in the town of The Dalles with salmonella bacteria, temporarily sickening 751 people with a diarrheal illness. The purpose of this covert attack was not to kill but rather to keep voters at home, with the aim of throwing the outcome of a local election in the cult's favor.

Although it is clear that urban society is vulnerable to chemical and biological terrorism, the probability of future mass-casualty incidents is harder to assess. Those groups capable of carrying out a catastrophic attack would have three characteristics: a motivation to kill large numbers of people indiscriminately; an organizational structure that would enable them to avoid premature detection and arrest; and the technical expertise and financial resources needed to produce and deliver chemical or biological agents effectively. Fortunately, terrorist groups rarely possess this combination of characteristics.

MOTIVATIONS

In 1989, Jeffrey Simon, a terrorism expert from RAND, published a hypothetical profile of a terrorist group most likely to resort to biological weapons.[1] In his view, such a group would lack a defined constituency and hence be unconcerned about political backlash; would have a track record of incidents that caused high casualties; would demonstrate a certain degree of technical sophistication and innovation in weaponry or tactics; and would have shown a willingness to take risks.

Simon's profile suggests that the types of terrorists most likely to resort to toxic weapons include religious or millenarian sects who believe that large-scale violence is a fulfillment of apocalyptic prophecy, brutalized ethnic minorities seeking revenge, and small terrorist cells driven by extremist ideologies or conspiracy theories. This "new breed" of terrorists is not motivated by a defined political agenda but by amorphous religious, racial, or antigovernment belief systems. They are potentially more prone to indiscriminate attacks because they have fluid objectives, perceive fewer political or moral constraints on the scope of their actions, may be interested in violence for its own sake, and are less easily deterred by threats of punishment. Disgruntled loners like Theodore Kaczynski (also known as the Unabomber, who is serving a life sentence for sending 16 mail bombs that killed 3 people and wounded 29 others) may also be motivated to employ toxic weapons, but technical and resource limitations would probably make them incapable of a mass-casualty attack.

In contrast, politically motivated terrorists generally operate at the level of violence sufficient to achieve their ends, while avoiding excessive or indiscriminate bloodshed that could alienate their supporters and provoke the full repressive power of government authorities. Traditional terrorist organizations also tend to be conservative and risk-averse with respect to their choice of weapons and tactics, relying on guns and explosives and innovating only when necessary.

These theoretical speculations are consistent with historical trends observed in the Monterey database. Most of the groups implicated in chemical or biological terrorism over the past century were not traditional, politically motivated terrorist organizations. Of the 101 documented attacks, 25 were perpetrated by religiously motivated groups, 17 by national-separatist groups, 8 by single-issue groups such as anti-abortion or animal-rights activists, 5 by lone actors, 3 by left-wing groups, and 2 by right-wing groups. (In the remaining 41 cases the perpetrators were unknown.)

In the volume *Toxic Terror,* detailed case studies of nine terrorist groups or individuals who acquired or used chemical or biological agents between 1946 and 1998 further suggest that "toxic terrorists" share a number of characteristics not seen in politically motivated terrorists.[2] The groups that acquired chemical or biological agents typically escalated their attacks over time, had, as Jeffrey Simon noted, no clearly defined base of political support, and believed they were fulfilling a divine command or prophecy that legitimated murder. These groups were motivated by a variety of perceived goals: destroying a corrupt social structure, fighting a tyrannical government, fulfilling an apocalyptic prophecy, punishing evil-doers or oppressors, or waging "defensive aggression" against outsiders seeking the destruction of the group.

In a few rare cases, a group's deep frustration or despair over the failure to achieve its objectives by conventional means, or the prospect of imminent arrest or extinction, has precipitated a resort to toxic weapons. In 1946, a group of Jewish Holocaust survivors calling themselves DIN (the Hebrew word for "justice" and also a Hebrew acronym for "Avenging Israel's Blood") sought retribution for the attempted Nazi extermination of the Jews by planning to poison the water supplies of major German cities. When this ambitious plan proved unworkable, members of the group secretly applied arsenic to the bread supply of a prisoner-of-war camp near Nuremberg that housed former SS officers, sickening a few thousand inmates.

The hothouse atmosphere present in a closed religious group led by a charismatic but authoritarian leader may also create psychological conditions conducive to extreme violence. Aum Shinrikyo, for example, sought to inflict mass casualties by releasing aerosols of anthrax bacteria or botulinum toxin in central Tokyo at least 10 times between 1990 and 1995 (fortunately, technical problems prevented the attacks from causing any known casualties). Cult leader Shoko Asahara's goal was to trigger social chaos, enabling the group to seize control of the Japanese government and impose a theocratic state. Aum even established a "shadow government" with a full set of ministries that were preparing to take power.

Despite these examples, the vast majority of chemical or biological terrorist incidents in the historical record do not involve attempts to inflict mass casualties but rather the tactical use of toxic weapons to kill or punish specific individuals. In 1991, for example, the Minnesota

Patriots Council, a right-wing tax-resistance group based in Alexandria, Minnesota, extracted ricin from castor beans purchased by mail order and conspired to use the poison to assassinate local police officers and federal officials. (The group's four leading members were arrested before they could carry out an attack.) Aum Shinrikyo operatives also employed nerve agents in several assassination attempts—some of which were successful—against individual defectors and critics. In a June 1994 incident in the central Japanese city of Matsumoto, cult members released a cloud of sarin gas near a dormitory housing three judges who were about to issue a legal judgment against the cult in a real estate case. The judges were injured in the attack, which killed 7 people and led to the hospitalization of about 200. In the case of the March 1995 Tokyo subway attack, the immediate target was the national police agency, with the aim of disrupting an imminent police raid on the cult's headquarters.

Finally, terrorists seeking to incapacitate many people without killing them might select a nonlethal chemical or biological agent but employ it indiscriminately, as in the Rajneeshee food-poisoning case. Thus, terrorist attacks with toxic weapons are potentially of four types: lethal/discriminate, lethal/indiscriminate, nonlethal/discriminate, and nonlethal/indiscriminate, with only a tiny minority of incidents likely to be in the much-feared lethal/indiscriminate category.

STRUCTURE

From an organizational perspective, a terrorist group capable of carrying out a large-scale chemical or biological attack would probably require most or all of the following characteristics: a charismatic leader who inspires total devotion and obedience; a set of technically skilled individuals who subscribe to the group's goals and ideology; a system of internal social controls that severely punish deviation or defection; and an organizational structure that resists penetration by police or intelligence agencies.

Most of the terrorist organizations in the United States that have sought to acquire chemical or biological agents have been stopped by local or federal law enforcement agencies before they could stage an effective attack. In 1972, for instance, an eco-terrorist group called RISE, which was led by two students at a community college in Chicago, plotted to wipe out the entire human race with eight different microbial pathogens and then repopulate the world with their own genes. They eventually scaled down their plans to contaminating urban water supplies in the Midwest. Before they could act, however, concerned group members told the FBI about the plot and the two ringleaders fled to Cuba.

cialized military response teams—the Army Technical Escort Unit and the Marine Corps Chemical-Biological Incident Response Force—are already in place.

Government programs for responding to chemical or biological terrorism should also be designed to be multipurpose rather than highly specialized, allowing them to offer social benefits regardless of how seriously one assesses the terrorist threat. For example, instead of developing specialized training courses for first responders, existing hazardous-materials (Hazmat) programs that train firefighters to clean up spills of toxic industrial chemicals should be expanded to cover deliberate releases of chemical warfare agents. Similarly, upgrading the ability of state and local public health departments to detect and contain outbreaks of infectious disease would greatly improve the nation's security, whether the cause of a given outbreak is natural or deliberate. By leveraging civil-defense programs in this manner, it should be possible to sustain public and congressional support for such efforts over the long run.

NOTES

1.   Jeffrey D. Simon, *Terrorists and the Potential Use of Biological Weapons: A Discussion of Possibilities* (Santa Monica, Calif.: RAND, December 1989), p. 17.

2.   Jonathan B. Tucker, ed., *Toxic Terror: Assessing Terrorist Use of Chemical and Biological Weapons* (Cambridge: MIT Press, 2000).

Reprinted with permission from *Current History* magazine (April 2000). © 2007 Current History, Inc.

A terrorist's preferred weapons are not complicated—guns, grenades, cars transformed into rolling bombs, or simply an explosive vest strapped around the torso of some suicidal "martyr." The vast majority of attacks carried out by al Qaeda, Hamas, and Hezbollah, among other groups, involve the use of common technologies that produce simple, often improvised weapons. Occasionally, more sophisticated devices such as mortars, rockets, or shoulder-fired missiles are employed, but these instances are rare. Al Qaeda's strike against the World Trade Center on September 11, 2001, was an exception that proved the rule. It stood out by reason of its technological complexity and meticulous planning. Yet even then, the weapons used to hijack the three airliners were surprisingly crude. True, the terrorists that day made guided missiles out of ordinary passenger planes, but the jets were first commandeered by men wielding arms no more high-tech than box cutters from a hardware store.

Terrorists, it seems, like to keep things uncomplicated. But the day may come when they change their minds, acquire a taste for more advanced arms, and switch to weapons of mass destruction. These are literally terror weapons, and among them none are more frightening than nuclear bombs. President George W. Bush spoke pointedly about nuclear explosives when he made it his administration's "highest priority . . . to keep terrorists from acquiring weapons of mass destruction."* Al Qaeda and similar organizations, the president said, had to be prevented from aquiring bombs that could conceivably blow up all or part of a major U.S. city.

Without a doubt, nuclear and radiological weapons occupy a dark and terrifying place in the popular imagination. People worry understandably that terrorists might somehow come into the possession of highly radioactive material or even a working nuclear bomb. The prospect of a nuclear blast or the detonation of a radiological "dirty bomb" in an American metropolis is troubling, but it is perhaps less likely than one would think. Gavin Cameron, the author of the next article, argued some years ago that it was not very likely at all. Cameron contended that the difficulties associated with nuclear terrorism almost eliminated it as a viable tactic. Though they loom large in nightmare scenarios of mass murder, Cameron concluded, nuclear and radiological weapons have much more psychological than actual strategic terror value.

NOTES

*   Graham Allison, "How to Stop Nuclear Terror," *Foreign Affairs* (January/February 2004). Available online, http://www.foreignaffairs.org/20040101faessay83107/graham-allison/how-to-stop-nuclear-terror.html (accessed December 7, 2006).

Nuclear Terrorism Reconsidered
GAVIN CAMERON

Fears about nuclear terrorism have a long history. It is now 25 years since Brian Jenkins wrote the seminal "Will Terrorists Go Nuclear?" which effectively launched the study of terrorism with weapons of mass destruction. Today the threat of nuclear terrorism has been subsumed by greater concerns over the use of chemical or biological weapons by terrorists. This is in part because nuclear terrorism is usually defined as the detonation of a nuclear-yield device, which, in turn, supposes that terrorists have the ability to steal an intact nuclear weapon or build a crude nuclear-yield device, both extremely difficult tasks. Yet it remains a real concern, as do two other types of action that should also be considered nuclear terrorism: attacks on nuclear reactors, and the dispersal of radiological materials. Both are more likely than the detonation of a nuclear-yield weapon, although they also would have significantly lesser consequences.

LOOSE NUKES AND SUITCASE BOMBS

Concerns over terrorist denotation of a nuclear-yield weapon have heightened significantly since the Soviet Union's collapse in 1991. These fears largely stem from the opportunities for nuclear materials and nuclear expertise to leave the country and be exploited by rogue states or terrorists. That terrorists could acquire an intact nuclear weapon (a so-called "loose nuke") seems far-fetched: states obviously have a considerable stake in protecting their mass-destruction weapons. Still, high-level allegations have been made that the whereabouts of an unspecified number of Soviet-era Atomic Demolition Munitions ("suitcase bombs") remain unknown. Given Russian denials, it has proved impossible to determine whether such weapons are missing—or whether they ever existed.

Two terrorist groups—the Japanese doomsday cult Aum Shinrikyo and al Qaeda, the network of suspected Saudi-born terrorist Osama bin Laden— unsuccessfully sought nuclear weapons in the former Soviet Union in the early 1990s. Given the wealth and contacts each possesses, their failure suggests that such acquisitions remain far from easy—even in the former Soviet bloc.

The belief that Russia or any other state might be willing to sponsor a client group to use a nuclear device against its enemies seems equally implausible. Fear of retribution from the attacked state and the international community, potential loss of control over the client group, and a reluctance to surrender the nuclear weapons to another party due to the intrinsic difficulty of acquiring them mitigate against such state sponsorship.

Another pathway to nuclear-yield terrorism is to acquire the material needed to construct a nuclear device. But gathering sufficient nuclear material is extremely difficult. Despite reports of nuclear "leakage" in the former Soviet Union, only a handful of cases involving weapons-significant materials are known, and date to the early 1990s. Never was the quantity involved sufficient to build a weapon. For example, after failing to acquire an intact nuclear weapon, al Qaeda sought to purchase fissile materials. Members of the group were offered what was described as highly enriched uranium (HEU), which was actually low-enriched uranium, and thus unusable in a nuclear weapon without extensive processing.

It would be unwise to assume that all terrorist groups would similarly fail, or that the former Soviet Union is the only place to seek nuclear materials. Aum Shinrikyo mined natural uranium in Australia in 1993 and sought to enrich it. But because most groups likely would be deterred by the cost, difficulty, and time required for material enrichment, Aum's example may prove unique.[1] The need to acquire a considerable quantity of fissile material would seem to preclude all but the most affluent or state-sponsored groups from crafting their own nuclear devices.

Terrorists seeking to build a nuclear weapon have two options: constructing a gun-type weapon using HEU, or developing an implosion device using either HEU or plutonium. Although the gun-type device has the simpler design of the two, it would require approximately 50 kilograms (kg) of HEU, an enormous quantity to acquire covertly on the black market. A gun-type device requires the firing of a less-than-critical mass quantity of HEU (about 15 kg) down a cylinder (the "gun barrel"), using a high-explosive charge, into another, less-than-critical mass quantity of HEU (about 40 kg) at the other end of the cylinder. The two quantities of uranium, combined, form a supercritical mass and thus cause a nuclear-yield explosion.

An implosion device would require approximately 8 kg of plutonium. The plutonium would then be machined into a sphere, surrounded by shaped high explosives, and detonated by a symmetrical shock wave. The difficulties arise in two areas: the sphere of plutonium must be minutely engineered, and the shock wave must be simultaneous to the millionth of a second. If either condition is not met, a substantial risk of an unpredictable nuclear yield or, more likely, a failure to reach super-criticality will occur. The risk of having a "fizzle" may not be a major deterrent to terrorist groups, however, since the effects still would be considerable, although less than those of a nuclear yield.

Indeed, the prestige associated with acquiring a nuclear capability is unmatched by chemical or biological weapons. A nuclear device would set a terrorist organization apart from any other group; would compel governments to take the terrorists seriously; and would represent a "quantum leap" in terrorist tactics. An effective nuclear-yield weapon would be unequaled in its potential, capable of wiping out entire cities.

This suggests that nuclear-yield weapons would be also be unsurpassed as terrorist instruments, and could be used to exact almost any demand. But a nuclear weapon would be difficult to use as a means of achieving certain terrorist objectives. If mass casualties were the sole aim, a nuclear-yield weapon would be effective. Such an attack, delivered without warning or demands, is the most plausible use of a nuclear-yield weapon by terrorists. For most other objectives, however, especially traditional political goals, a nuclear weapon would be disproportionate and counterproductive; such destruction could alienate a group's constituency and bring the full weight of the targeted state's counterterrorism effort down on it. Credibility is also a vital factor: the targeted state would have to believe that the terrorist group might use its weapon. Few realistic demands would seem serious enough to justify such a threat. Finally, there is the issue of achieving long-term objectives: any state is likely to require that the terrorists surrender their nuclear weapon as part of a deal. Once that happens, do the terrorists require a second device to prevent the state from reneging?

Another possibility is a credible hoax. As a means of achieving political goals or causing disruption, a credible hoax is likely to be as effective as genuinely possessing the weapon. Although a genuine terrorist incident involving a nuclear-yield weapon has never occurred, hoaxes and groups expressing interest in such weapons abound. But this too would be difficult to execute properly. The United States government has a centralized database of previous threats and descriptions of open-source technical information that permit rapid credibility assessment. Achieving a convincing threat would not require obtaining fissile materials or constructing a weapon, but would demand an in-depth knowledge of nuclear weapons.

TARGETING REACTORS

Another major source of concern, especially in the United States, is terrorist targeting of nuclear reactors. Reactors are potentially attractive targets for terrorists since they offer a means for a group to achieve a spectacular attack that sets it apart from other groups and ensures that it is noticed as an organization. Possible motivations that might lead terrorists to consider such an attack include blackmail through a barricade-and-hostage situation; theft of strategic nuclear material (either as a prelude to a radiological attack or as part of an effort to develop a nuclear capability); or, destruction of the reactor itself.

In the West, most actions directed against reactors have been motivated by antinuclear politics, the sites chosen because such plants represent high-profile targets. Antinuclear actions have been characterized by a preference for attacking property rather than people, a tendency common in single-issue terrorism. In November 1987 a bomb planted outside Lawrence Livermore National Laboratory in California shattered windows and damaged cars but did not cause any injuries. The Nuclear Liberation Front claimed responsibility for the attack at the facility, which provided support for the United States nuclear program. In January 1982 five antitank rockets were fired at a partially built reactor near Lyon, France, slightly damaging the outer building. A previously unknown group, the Pacifist and Ecologist Committee, claimed responsibility for the attack.

The majority of antinuclear campaigns are intrinsically demonstration actions, aimed at displaying the ineffective safety and security of nuclear installations and materials. Their purpose is to highlight the danger posed by the plant and to interfere with its operations. Antinuclear groups are unlikely to threaten the integrity of the reactor, for fear of sparking the type of incident that they most fear. Groups whose primary motivation is ecological are also extremely unlikely to seek results that would damage the environment.

Reactor attacks directed against high-profile targets have been motivated by both political and economic considerations. The guerrilla group Basque Homeland and Freedom (ETA), perhaps more than any other politically motivated terrorist group, has targeted reactors. In March 1981 ETA sent death threats to 33 technicians working at the Lemoniz nuclear power plant in Spain. The threats had little impact: the technicians continued working at the plant, even in the wake of the assassinations of the chief engineer in January 1981 and the project manager in May 1982.

The economic and political instability in the former Soviet Union has also caused an increased threat of attacks on the nuclear facilities themselves. Since 1992 at least five attacks or credible threats have been directed against reactors in the post-Soviet states. Chechen rebels, for example, have made repeated threats against reactors in Russia. And in November 1994, Kestutis Mazuika, a Lithuanian national in Sweden, threatened to destroy the facility at Ignalina, Lithuania unless a ransom of $8 million was paid to a secret organization (NUC-41 W), which he claimed to represent. The group is also thought to have been responsible for the theft of fuel rods from the same facility in 1993.

One threat that has historically caused widespread concern, especially in the United States, is the vulnerability of nuclear facilities to truck bombs. Other forms of frontal assault on reactors by terrorists have a low probability of success— especially releasing radiation—largely because reactors are not only well defended but can also be shut down from several locations. Still, if terrorists were to succeed in destroying or disabling both the backup and the primary coolant systems at a reactor, they might cause a core meltdown, even if the reactor was shut down.

Nuclear reactors are not the only parts of the nuclear complex that are vulnerable to attack; enrichment, storage, and spent-fuel reprocessing facilities are also potential targets. Spent fuel is seemingly at its most vulnerable during transport. But because spent fuel is shipped in casks that protect the public from radiation, the construction of these casks is extremely robust. A truck bomb or shaped explosive would prove incapable of causing a significant leak.

RADIOLOGICAL TERRORISM

If terrorists were able to damage severely the containment system of a nuclear reactor, especially in the early stages of an attack, it would greatly increase their chances of achieving an off-site radiological dispersal. Smaller quantities of radioactive material could also be used as a terrorist weapon. Even low-grade nuclear material would have considerable utility as the basis for a radiological terrorist device. Materials in this category can be more easily stolen from nuclear, industrial, and research facilities than weapons-grade material. A radiological device would be extremely easy to construct (it need only be an aerosol can, a bomb with a radioactive coating, or a bomb placed alongside a container of radioactive substance), and the materials for it are widely available (cesium-137, for example, is commonly used in hospitals for x-rays). Certain elements, such as cesium and cobalt-60, which need intense fire to disperse them effectively, could be used in radiological weapons if the substance was surrounding a mixture of high explosive and incendiary material. While a firebomb of this variety is technologically well within the reach of many terrorist organizations, a group might also consider using military munitions for this purpose.

The technical feasibility of radiological terrorism make it by far the most likely form of nuclear weapon. Although it is the least catastrophic, a radiological device would still have considerable value as a terrorist weapon since its nuclear component would almost certainly ensure a considerable impact on the public's imagination and fear—and thus on government response. Radiological weapons would, like nuclear-yield weapons, set a group apart and take its terrorism to a different level.

The use of a radiological weapon would be more difficult than most "off the shelf" weaponry and would require technological innovation by terrorist groups. Unlike a nuclear-yield bomb, however, which is an extremely expensive and difficult mass-casualty weapon, a radiological device would be only moderately difficult to build and use and would inflict few casualties. These differences are critical in the ability and willingness of terrorists to justify its use. As such, radiological weapons would represent a less radical break with traditional terrorist tactics, and are therefore more plausible than a nuclear-yield bomb.

It is almost impossible to generalize on the extent of the risk to the public from a radiological dispersal device: damage would depend on the means of dispersal, population density, weather conditions, and the period of public exposure. Most important, the effects of a radiological weapon are related to the type of material used: while weapons-grade plutonium might cause limited damage, other elements, such as cesium, or even radioactive waste, are potentially lethal in a short period of time. Nevertheless, radiological devices are not ideal for causing mass casualties because the vast quantities of highly radioactive material required to cause powerful results over even a moderate area would pose considerable problems for terrorists to acquire and then use it. Moreover, the majority of health effects of radiological weapons are likely to be long-term. Most groups would want more immediate dramatic effects and are unlikely see the utility of an increased incidence of cancers decades after their attack.

date or coerce people." "We shall define cyberterrorism as any act of terrorism . . . that uses information systems or computer technology either as a *weapon* or a *target*," stated a recent NATO brief, *Technology and Terrorism*. Yael Shahar, webmaster at the International Policy Institute for Counter-Terrorism in Herzliya, Israel, differentiates between many different types of what he prefers to call "information terrorism": "electronic warfare" occurs when hardware is the target, "psychological warfare" is the goal of inflammatory content, and only "hacker warfare," according to Shahar, degenerates into cyberterrorism.

John Leyden, writing in *The Register*, describes how a group of Palestinian hackers and sympathizers set up a web site that provides one-stop access to hacking tools and viruses, and tips on how to use these tools to mount attacks on Israeli targets. According to Leyden, these hackers are using the techniques of cyberterrorism.[3] It is clear that Leyden and others wish to conflate politically motivated hacking—so-called hacktivism—and terrorism. Advancing one step further, Johan J. Ingles-le Noble, in the October 21, 1999 *Jane's Intelligence Review*, wrote that "Cyberterrorism is not only about damaging systems but also about intelligence gathering. The intense focus on 'shut-down-the-power-grid' scenarios and tight analogies with physically violent techniques ignore other more potentially effective uses of IT [information technology] in terrorist warfare: intelligence-gathering, counter-intelligence and disinformation."

Ingles-le Noble's comments highlight the more potentially realistic and effective uses of the Internet by terrorist groups. He mistakenly labels these alternative uses "cyberterrorism." Such a taxonomy is unnecessary. Consider the November 2000 electronic attack carried out from Pakistan against the American Israel Public Affairs Committee (AIPAC), a pro-Israeli lobbying group in Washington, D.C. The group's site was defaced with anti-Israeli commentary. The attacker also stole some 3,500 e-mail addresses and 700 credit card numbers, sent anti-Israeli diatribes to the addresses, and published the credit card data on the Internet. The Pakistani hacker who claimed responsibility for the incident, the self-styled Dr. Nuker, said he was a founder of the Pakistani Hackerz Club, the aim of which was to "hack for the injustice going around the globe, especially with [sic] Muslims."[4] Even had Dr. Nuker physically broken into AIPAC's headquarters and stolen the credit card information and e-mail addresses, it would be considered a criminal undertaking, not an act of terrorism. Only if an individual like Dr. Noble used the information to perpetrate a violent attack in furtherance of some political aim would his or her actions be considered terrorist.

Ingles-le Noble further contends that "disinformation is easily spread; rumors get picked up by the media, aided by the occasional anonymous e-mail." That may be so, but spreading false information, whether by way of word-of-mouth, the print or broadcast media, or some other medium, is often not even criminal, let alone terrorist. Why should it be any different in cyberspace? Ingles-le Noble himself recognizes that "there is undoubtedly a lot of exaggeration in this field. If your system goes down, it is a lot more interesting to say it was the work of a foreign government rather than admit it was due to an American teenage 'script-kiddy' tinkering with a badly written CGI [computer-generated imagery] script. If the power goes out, people light a candle and wait for it to return, but do not feel terrified. If their mobile phones switch off, society does not instantly feel under attack. If someone cracks a web site and changes the content, terror does not stalk the streets."

In February 2001, Britain updated its Terrorism Act to classify the "use of or threat of action that is designed to seriously interfere with or seriously disrupt an electronic system" as an act of terrorism. Police investigators will decide whether an action is to be regarded as terrorist. On-line groups, human rights organizations, civil liberties campaigners, and others condemned this classification as absurd, pointing out that it placed hacktivism on a par with life-threatening acts of public intimidation.[5]

In the wake of September 11, American legislators followed suit. Previously, if one successfully infiltrated a federal computer network, one was considered a hacker. Following the passage of the USA Patriot Act, however, which grants significant powers to law enforcement agencies to investigate and prosecute potential threats to national security, hackers can be labeled cyberterrorists and, if convicted, face up to 20 years in prison.[6] Clearly, policymakers believe that actions taken in cyberspace are qualitatively different from those taken in the "real" world.

"USE" AND "MISUSE" OF THE INTERNET

Cybercrime and cyberterrorism are not coterminous. Cyberspace attacks must have a "terrorist" component to be labeled cyberterrorism. The attacks must instill terror as commonly understood (that is, result in death or large-scale destruction), and they must have a political motivation.

As for terrorist use of information technology and terrorism involving computer technology as a weapon/target, only the latter may be defined as cyberterrorism. Terrorists' "use" of computers as a facilitator of their activities, whether for propaganda, communication, or other purposes, is simply that: "use." And the vast majority of terrorist activity on the Internet is limited to "use."

Researchers are still unclear whether the ability to communicate on-line worldwide has resulted in an increase or a decrease in terrorist acts. They agree, however, that on-line activities substantially improve the ability of such terrorist groups to raise funds, lure new faithful, and reach a mass audience. The most popular terrorist sites draw tens of thousands of visitors each month.

Hezbollah—a Lebanese-based Shiite Islamic group also known as Islamic Jihad, the Revolutionary Justice Organization, Organization of the Oppressed on Earth, and Islamic Jihad for the Liberation of Palestine—established its collection of web sites in 1995. The group currently manages three such sites: one for its press office, another to describe its attacks on Israeli targets (accessible at <http://www.moqawama.tv>), and a third, Al-Manar TV, for news and information (on-line at <http://www.manartv.com>). All three may be viewed in either English or Arabic. The central press office site contains an introduction to the group, press clippings and statements, political declarations, and speeches of the group's secretary general. One may also access a photo gallery and video and audio clips. The information contained in these pages is updated regularly. Contact information, in the form of an e-mail address, is provided.

In a similar vein, the web site of Hamas, the Palestinian militant Islamic fundamentalist group, which is currently off-line, presents political cartoons, streaming video clips, and photomontages depicting the violent deaths of Palestinian children. It has been claimed that the Armed Islamic Group (GIA), a fundamentalist sect warring with the Algerian government, posted a detailed bomb-making manual on the Hamas site. The on-line home of the Liberation Tigers of Tamil Eelam (LTTE), a guerrilla force in Sri Lanka best known for the 1991 assassination of former Indian Prime Minister Rajiv Ghandi, offers position papers, daily news, an online store—for sale are books and pamphlets, videos, audiotapes, CDs, a 2002 calendar, and the Tamil Eelam flag—and free e-mail services. Other terrorist sites host electronic bulletin boards, post tips on smuggling money to finance their operations, and provide automated registration for e-mail alerts.

Many terrorist groups' sites are hosted in the United States. For example, a Connecticut-based Internet service provider (ISP) was providing co-location and virtual hosting services for the Hamas site in data centers located in Connecticut and Chicago. While sites such as that maintained by Hamas are likely to receive more intense scrutiny following the September attacks, similar web sites were the subject of debate in the United States prior to the events of September 11. In 1997 controversy erupted when it was revealed that the State University of New York at Binghamton was hosting the web site of the Revolutionary Armed Forces of Colombia (FARC), and that a solidarity site for the Peruvian guerrilla group Tupac Amaru (MRTA) was operating out of the University of California at San Diego. Officials at the State University of New York promptly shut down the FARC site. In San Diego it was decided to err on the side of free speech and allow the Tupac Amaru site son with such targeted and to remain open.[7] (The FARC sustained campaigns. The site now also operates out of the University of California at San Diego.) Hosting such a site is not illegal— even if a group is deemed a foreign terrorist organization by the United States State Department— as long as a site is not seeking financial contributions or providing financial support to the group. Other content is generally considered to be protected speech under the First Amendment of the Constitution.

It is not all clear sailing for these "netizens," however. Their home pages have been subject to intermittent denial of service and other hack attacks, and strikes against their ISPs have resulted in more permanent difficulties. In 1997, for example, an e-mail bombing was conducted against the Institute for Global Communications (IGC), a San Francisco–based ISP hosting the web pages of the *Euskal Herria* or *Basque Country Journal,* a publication edited by supporters of the Basque group Homeland and Liberty (ETA). The attacks against IGC commenced following the assassination by the ETA of a popular town councilor in northern Spain. The protesters hoped to pull the site from the Internet. To accomplish this they bombarded IGC with thousands of spurious e-mails routed through hundreds of different mail relays, spammed IGC staff and customer accounts, clogged their web page with false credit card orders, and threatened to employ the same tactics against other organizations using IGC services. IGC pulled the *Euskal Herria* site on July 18, but not before archiving a copy of the site. Shortly thereafter, mirror sites appeared on half a dozen servers on three continents. Despite this, the protesters' e-mail action raised fears of a new era of censorship imposed by direct action from anonymous hacktivists. Furthermore, approximately one month after IGC pulled the controversial site off its servers, Scotland Yard's Anti-Terrorist Branch shut down Internet Freedom's British web site for hosting the journal. Scotland Yard claimed to be acting against terrorism.

The so-called cyberwar that raged between Israelis and Palestinians and their supporters in 2000 was a mere nuisance in comparison with such targeted and sustained campaigns. The Middle East "cyberwar" began in October, about three weeks after Hezbollah seized three Israeli soldiers on patrol in the Shebaa Farms area of southern Lebanon and held them for ransom. Pro-Israeli hackers created a web site to host attacks. Within days, Hezbollah's site was flooded by millions of "pings"—the cyberequivalent of knocks on the door—and crashed. Hezbollah then tried to revive the site under slightly different spellings, but they too came under sustained attack. In all, six different Hezbollah sites, the Hamas site, and other Palestinian informational sites were victims of the attack. Hezbollah's central press office site came under attack once again when the group posted video clips of Israeli ground attacks on Palestinians in Gaza. Hezbollah then increased its server capacity to ward off further attacks. These efforts notwithstanding, pro-Israeli hackers successfully hacked into the Hezbollah web site a further time on December 26. They posted pictures of the three Israeli soldiers who were abducted in early October and the slogan "Free Our Soldiers Now" on a screen full of blue-and-white Star of David flags.

According to Hezbollah's then webmaster, Ali Ayoub, "Our counterattack is just to remain on the net." The Palestinians and their supporters were not long in striking back, however. In a coordinated counterattack, the web sites of the Israeli army, Foreign Ministry, prime minister, and parliament, among others, were hit. On December 29, 80 Israeli-related sites were hacked and defaced by pro-Palestinian hackers. More than 246 Israeli-related sites were estimated to have been attacked between October 6, 2000 and January 1, 2001 (compared with approximately 34 Palestinian-related sites that were hit in the same period). The success of the Palestinian counterattack—variously dubbed the "ejihad," "cyberjihad," or "inter-fada"—may be explained by the way in which the pro-Palestinian hackers systematically worked their way through sites with .il domain names. Palestinian-related sites are generally harder to find because only one such domain is currently operational (gov.ps) and few groups have such easily identifiable Internet addresses, or URLs (uniform resource locators), as Hezbollah. In addition, Israel has approximately 2 million Internet hookups, considerably more than in any other Middle Eastern country. The upshot is that the Israelis have a far greater on-line presence than the Palestinians and are therefore more easily targeted. In addition, in mid-July 2002, accessing the Internet in the West Bank and Gaza became all but impossible when the Israel Defense Forces shut down Palnet, the leading Palestinian ISP.

HIDDEN IN PLAIN SIGHT

In a briefing given in late September 2002, FBI Assistant Director Ronald Dick, head of the United States National Infrastructure

Protection Center, told reporters that the hijackers had used the net, and "used it well." The Internet and the abilities of intelligence officials to eavesdrop on e-mail and phone calls was supposed to help prevent attacks such as those that occurred in New York and Washington. They did not and, as a result, assumptions about the role the Internet can play in fighting terrorism are being challenged. Investigators are nevertheless relying on Internet tools as never before. What role has the Internet played in the investigation of the attacks thus far? What can be done on-line to track the group depends in large part on what it did on-line.

In the immediate aftermath of the attacks, federal agents issued subpoenas and search warrants to nearly every major Internet-related company, including America Online, Microsoft, Yahoo!, Google, and many smaller providers. It is known that the hijackers booked at least nine of their airline tickets for the four doomed flights on-line at least two to three weeks prior to the attacks. They also used the Internet to find information about the aerial application of pesticides. Investigators are said to have in their possession hundreds of e-mails linked to the terrorists in English, Arabic, and Urdu. The messages were sent within the United States and internationally. According to the FBI, many of these messages include operational details of the attacks. Some of the hijackers used e-mail services that are largely anonymous—Hotmail, for example—and created multiple temporary accounts. A number of them are known to have used public terminals, in libraries and elsewhere, to gain access to the net, whereas others used privately owned personal or laptop computers.

In two successive briefings, senior FBI officials stated that the agency had found no evidence that the hijackers used electronic encryption methods to communicate on the Internet. This has not, however, prevented politicians and journalists from repeating lurid rumors that the coded orders for the attacks were secretly hidden inside pornographic web images or from making claims that the attacks could have been prevented had Western governments been given the power to prevent Internet users from employing encryption in their communications.[8] Although many e-mail messages sent to and from key members of the hijack teams were uncovered and studied, none of them, according to the FBI, used encryption. Nor did they use steganography, a technique that allows an encrypted file to be hidden inside a larger file (such as a JPEG or GIF image, or an MP3 music file). Evidence from questioning terrorists involved in previous attacks, both in America and on American interests abroad, and monitoring their messages reveals that they simply used code words to make their communications appear innocuous to eavesdroppers.

AFTER SEPTEMBER 11

Authorities have been keeping a watchful eye on web sites perceived as extremist for a number of years. In February 1998, Dale Watson, chief of the international terrorism section of the FBI, informed the United States Senate judiciary committee that major terrorist groups used the Internet to spread propaganda and recruit new members. Before September 11, however, the authorities were prohibited legally from interfering with such sites. The FBI has since been involved in the official closure of what appears to be hundreds—if not thousands—of sites. Several radical Internet radio shows, including "IRA Radio," "Al Lewis Live," and "Our Americas," were pulled by an Indiana ISP in late September 2001 after being advised by the FBI that their assets could be seized for promoting terrorism. The New York–based "IRA Radio" was accused of supporting the Real IRA. The site contained an archive of weekly radio programs said to back the dissident Irish guerrillas. The archive of political interviews from "Al Lewis Live," hosted by iconoclastic actor/activist Lewis (formerly "Grandpa" on the 1960s hit television show "The Munsters"), drew some 15,000 hits a day. "Our Americas" was a Spanish-language program about rebels in Latin America. Yahoo! has pulled dozens of sites in the "jihad web ring," a collection of 55 *jihad*-related sites, while Lycos Europe established a 20-person team to monitor its web sites for illegal activity and to remove terrorist-related content.

In August 2001 the Taliban outlawed the use of the Internet in Afghanistan, except at the fundamentalist group's headquarters. The Taliban nevertheless maintained a prominent home on the Internet despite UN sanctions, retaliatory hack attacks, and the vagaries of the United States bombing campaign. Before it went off-line, a site called Taliban Online contained information instructions on how to make financial donations, or donations of food and clothing, to the Afghan militia. The unofficial web site of Dharb-i-Mumin, a Taliban-associated organization the United States has put on a list of terrorist groups, is still operational at <http://dharb-i-mumin.cjb.net/>, although a United States–based web site operated by the group was shut down in late September 2001 following a request from the Treasury Department to the group's Kansas City–based ISP.

One of the larger jihad-related sites still in operation is Azzam.com, run by London-based Azzam Publications.[9] The Azzam site is available in more than a dozen languages and offers primers that include "How Can I Train Myself for *Jihad?*" Many Azzam affiliates were shut down after the ISPs hosting the sites received complaints (at least one following a request from the FBI). The British company Swift Internet, which was the technical and billing contact for an Azzam site, is said to have received threatening e-mails accusing it of supporting a terrorist web site. Swift has since distanced itself from the site by removing its name as a contact on public Internet records. Meanwhile, as often as the site is shut down, it is replaced by a substitute/mirror site under a different URL. According to an Azzam spokesperson, "One cannot shut down the Internet."

United States officials are said to be searching the Internet for the reappearance of an Arabic-language web site that they believe has been used by Al Qaeda. Statements ostensibly made by Al Qaeda and Taliban members have appeared on Alneda.com.[10] The site, which is registered in Singapore, appeared on web servers in Malaysia and Texas in early June 2002, before it was shut down by United States officials. It is thought to have first appeared on the net in early February 2002. It is expected to reappear under a numerical address in an effort to make it harder to track. According to media accounts, the site contained audio and video clips of Osama bin Laden; pictures of Al Qaeda suspects currently detained in Pakistan; a message purportedly from Al Qaeda spokesman Sulaiman Abu Ghaith, in which he warned of new attacks on the United States; and a series of articles claiming that suicide bombings aimed at Americans are justifiable under Islamic law. There has been media speculation that the site is being used to direct Al Qaeda operational cells. According to one report, the site has carried low-level operational information: in February it published the names and home telephone numbers of Al Qaeda fighters captured by Pakistan following their escape from fighting in Afghanistan with the hope that sympathizers would contact their families and let them know they were alive. Click on the link to Alneda.com today and the following appears: "Hacked, Tracked, and NOW Owned by the U.S.A." The site is described as a "mostly unmoderated discussion board relating to current world affairs surrounding Islamic Jihad [sic] and the United States led war on terrorism (plus other conflicts around the globe)."

BOMBS, NOT BYTES

Richard Clarke, White House special adviser for cyberspace security, has said that he prefers not to use the term "cyberterrorism" and favors instead "information security" or "cyberspace security" because, as he has noted, most terrorist groups have not engaged in information warfare (read "cyberterrorism"). Terrorist groups, he notes, have at this stage used the Internet only for propaganda, communications, and fundraising. In a similar vein, Michael Vatis, former head of the United States National Infrastructure Protection Center, has stated that "terrorists are already using technology for sophisticated communications and fund-raising activities. As yet we haven't seen computers being used by these groups as weapons to any significant degree, but this will probably happen in the future." According to a recent study, 75 percent of Internet users worldwide agree; they believe that "cyberterrorists" will "soon inflict massive casualties on innocent lives by attacking corporate and governmental computer networks." The survey, conducted in 19 major cities around the world, found that 45 percent of respondents agreed completely that "computer terrorism will be a growing problem," and another 35 percent agreed somewhat with the same state-ment.[11] The problem certainly cannot shrink much, hovering as it does at zero cyberterrorism incidents per year. This is not to say that cyberterrorism cannot or will not happen, but that, contrary to popular perception, it has not happened yet.

On Wednesday morning, September 12, 2001, an Internet user could still visit a web site that integrated three wonders of modern technology: the Internet, digital live video, and New York City's World Trade Center. The site allowed Internet users worldwide to appreciate what millions of tourists had thrilled to since Minoru Yamasaki's architectural wonder was completed in 1973: the stunning 45-mile view from the top of the Trade Center towers. According to journalists, the caption on the site still read "Real-Time Hudson River View from World Trade Center." In the square above was a deep black nothingness. The terrorists had taken down the towers; they had not taken down the Internet. As Dorothy Denning noted just weeks before the September attacks in the summer 2001 issue of *Harvard International Review,* "whereas hacktivism is real and widespread, cyberterrorism exists only in theory. Terrorist groups are using the Internet, but they still prefer bombs to bytes as a means of inciting terror." Terrorist "use" of the Internet has been largely ignored in favor of the more headline-grabbing "cyberterrorism."

NOTES

1. On May 3, 2002, the European Union updated its list of prohibited organizations. See <http://ue.eu.int/pressData/en/misc/70413.pdf>.

2. This definition is from Title 22 of the United States Code, Section 2656f(d). This is also the definition employed in the United States State Department's annual report *Patterns of Global Terrorism.*

3. See John Leyden, "Palestinian Crackers Give Out Tools to Attack Israelis," *The Register,* December 4, 2000 <http://www.theregister. co.uk/content/6/15199.html>.

4. Dr. Nuker's home page is at <http://clik.to/gett>. You must contact him by e-mail, however, to receive a password to enter the site.

5. Furthermore, Internet service providers in the United Kingdom may be legally required to monitor some customers' surfing habits if requested to do so by the police under the Regulation of Investigatory Powers Act 2000.

6. The Uniting and Strengthening America by Providing Appropriate Tools Required to Intercept and Obstruct Terrorism (USA PATRIOT) Act of 2001 was signed into law by President George W. Bush in October 2001. The law gives government investigators broad powers to track wireless phone calls, listen to voicemail, intercept e-mail messages, and monitor computer use. The full text of the act is available at <http://www.ins.usdoj.gov/graphics/lawsregs/ patriot.pdf>.

7. The Tupac Amaru Revolutionary Movement Solidarity Page hosted by the University of California at San Diego is at <http://burn. ucsd.edu/~ats/mrta.htm>. The official home page of the MRTA (in Europe) may be accessed at <http://www.voz-rebelde.de> and is available in English, Spanish, Italian, Japanese, Turkish, and Serbo-Croat.

8. In Britain, Foreign Secretary Jack Straw provoked a storm of protest by suggesting on national television that the media and civil liberties campaigners had paved the way for the terror attacks on America by advocating free speech and favoring publicly available encryption.

9. The site <http://www.azzam.com> is accessible intermittently. Qoqaz.net <http://www.qoqaz.net> is an Azzam mirror, as is <http:// www.azzam.co.uk>. If none of these sites is on-line, information on Azzam's new location might be found on the site <http://www.mak-tabah.net/home.asp>.

10. The site has also appeared at <http://www.drasat.com>.

11. Kevin Poulsen, "Cyber Terror in the Air," SecurityFocus.com, June 30, 2001.

Reprinted with permission from *Current History* magazine (December 2002). © 2007 Current History, Inc.

Why Do They Do It?

If it is difficult to say exactly who terrorists are, it is even harder to discern the motivations that are behind their actions. It is no easy matter to untangle the mass of psychological, social, and cultural factors that drive terrorists to kill and to willingly accept the likelihood of being killed. Any number of things contributes to the terrorist mind-set, a way of thinking that includes a total disregard for innocent human life in the service of a "cause." Seeking the source of terrorism in radical politics is insufficient; not all radicals turn to violence to make their points. Opposition to repressive government policies is likewise an inadequate explanation. The power of the state is often challenged and occasionally even undermined by nonviolent efforts at reform. The question, therefore, remains: why do people choose acts of terror as a form of political action? Scholar Martha Crenshaw, who has studied extremism in depth, has posed the same question this way: "Why is terrorism attractive to some opponents of the state, but unattractive to others?"* Why, in other words, is a conscious choice made to terrorize?

According to the 2005 U.S. Army training manual on terrorism, the reasons vary from personal gain to group dynamics. The motivations are as diverse as the practitioners of terror themselves. In every case, a suite of factors comes into play, each one making the use of terror acceptable, or even desirable. Different motivations also determine how terrorists plan and execute their attacks. No two terror operations, then, are ever the same. Groups and individual extremists choose their weapons and targets for reasons known best only to themselves; however, at least attempting to figure out what moves terrorists to do what they do is vital to the development of effective countermeasures and to saving lives in the process.

NOTES

* Martha Crenshaw, "The Logic of Terrorism: Terrorist Behavior as a Product of Strategic Choice," in *Origins Of Terror: Psychologies, Ideologies, Theologies, States of Mind*, ed. Walter Reich, 10 (Washington, D.C.: Woodrow Wilson Center Press, 1998).

Terrorist Behaviors and Motivations
THE U.S. ARMY TRAINING
AND DOCTRINE COMMAND

Terrorists and terror groups constitute the enemy in the current Global War on Terrorism the United States finds itself engaged in today. However, despite decades of study, the nature of terrorists and their behaviors are a wide ranging set of data. In addition to the difficulty in analyzing secretive, conspiratorial groups and individuals, the variety of motivations, ideologies, and behaviors involved are diverse. Common characteristics or clearly defined traits may be apparent in simplistic comparison, but significant contrasts are more the norm.

Yet, there are benefits to studying terrorist motivations and behaviors, both at the individual and group level. Observations on human nature and group dynamics under the conditions of stress, excitement, and social isolation can give insight into the causes of particular behaviors. Also, understanding the various types of motivations for particular terrorists allows assessment of stated aims against their actual intent.

This chapter is organized into three sections. The first section is a discussion of terrorist behaviors and psychology at both individual and group level. The second examines the impact of group goals and motivations on their planning and operations. The third section consists of observations of general terrorist characteristics.

SECTION I: TERRORIST BEHAVIOR

A common view of the terrorist is usually the unpredictable, viciously irrational stereotype emphasized by media images and sensationalism. However, as our examination of the nature and history of terrorism in Chapter 1 shows, terrorism is a rationally selected tactic, employed in the pursuit of political aims. To lend some truth to the cinema stereotype, individuals or small organizations that employ terrorist tactics may not always be concerned with particular causes or avowed ideology. Some terrorists may be motivated purely by a need to be terrorists, in whatever cause suits them, or as a "gun for hire" serving a variety of causes.

This contradiction is summed up in the two most common approaches in analyzing terrorist group and individual behavior. They are:

- The psychologically compelled (sociopath or psychopath) model: This supposes that terrorists engage in terrorism because it fulfills a psychological need (not exclusively a need for violence) on their part. This terrorism treats avowed ideology and political causes, as after the fact justifications for behaviors the terrorist will commit anyway.
- The rational choice model. Terror is a tactic selected after rational consideration of the costs and benefits in order to achieve an objective. The individual chooses participation in terrorist activities by a conscious decision (although they may not know what they are getting into). While it acknowledges that individuals or groups may be predisposed to violence, this is not considered the determining factor in the choice to use or renounce terror.

Neither of these descriptions is universally applicable, with all groups or individuals conforming to one or the other. Aspects of both theories are observed in groups and individuals. As usual, the real world provides instances of both theories, and they should both be kept in mind when examining the actions of terrorists.[1]

Individual Terrorist Behaviors

An opinion can be argued with; a conviction is best shot.
                                        T.E. Lawrence (of Arabia)

No one profile exists for terrorists in terms of their backgrounds or personal characteristics. The differences in the origins of terrorists in terms of their society, culture, and environment preclude such a universal approach for foreign or domestic terrorists. The profiles developed for the typical West German Red Army Faction (RAF) member 15 years ago is irrelevant to predicting the nature of an Indonesian al Qaeda recruit. Trying to predicatively profile potential terrorists, even within the same culture, is a task beyond the scope of this work.

UTOPIAN WORLDVIEW

...the time after victory, that is not our concern ...
We build the revolution, not the socialist model.
                Gudrun Ensslin, co-leader, Red Army Faction

Terrorists typically have utopian goals, regardless of whether their aims are political, social, territorial, nationalistic, or religious. This utopianism expresses itself forcefully as an extreme degree of impatience with the rest of the world that validates the terrorists' extreme methods.[2] This philosophy may be best expressed as "Tear everything up; change now and fix later." The individual commonly perceives a crisis too urgent to be solved other than by the most extreme methods. Alternately, the perception is of a system too corrupt or ineffective to see or adopt the "solution" the terrorist expounds. This sense of desperate impatience with opposition is central to the terrorist worldview. This is true of both secular and religiously motivated terrorists, although with slightly different perspectives as to how to impose their "solutions."

There is also a significant impractical element of associated with this utopian mindset. Although their goals often involve the transformation of society or a significant reordering of the status quo, individual terrorists—even the philosophical or intellectual leaders—are often vague or uncaring as to what the future order of things will look like or how aims will be implemented. Change, and the destructive method by which change is brought about, may be much more important than the end result.

INTERACTION WITH OTHERS Terrorists interact within their groups with both other members and leadership. It is common for individuals forming or joining groups to adopt the "leader principle." This amounts to unquestioning submission to the group's authority figure. This is true of both hierarchical and networked organizations, and of large or small groups. It explains the prevalence of individual leaders of great charisma in many terrorist organizations.[3] With a predisposition to view leaders and authority figures within the group as near ideal examples, such leaders can demand tremendous sacrifices from subordinates. This type of obedience can cause internal dissension when a leader is at odds with the group, or factions arise in the organization.[4]

Another adaptation the individual makes is accepting an "in-group" [us against the world] mentality. This results in a presumption of automatic morality on the part of the other individual members of the group, and the purity of their cause and righteousness of their goals. The view of the wider world may be perceived as aggressively attacking or persecuting the individual and his compatriots. Thus, violence is necessary for the "self-defense" of the group and carries moral justification. In some cases, the group comes to identify completely with their use of violence, and it becomes to them the defining characteristic of their existence on both the individual and collective level. Groups in this mind-set cannot renounce violence, since it would equal renouncing their own reason for being.[5]

DE-HUMANIZATION OF NON-MEMBERS

Dear animal killing scum! Hope we sliced your finger
wide open and that you now die from the rat poison
we smeared on the razor blade.
Anonymous letter rigged with rat poison-covered razor blades sent
to 65 guide outfitters across British Columbia and Alberta from the
"Justice Department" (radical animal rights group), January 1996

There is a de-humanization of all "out-group" individuals. This de-humanization permits violence to be directed indiscriminately at any target outside the group. Assuming that all those outside of the group are either enemies or neutral, terrorists are justified in attacking anyone. And since anyone outside the group is a potential enemy, circumstances can change that permit any restraints that the terrorists might have observed to be broken in the name of expediency.

De-humanization also removes some of the onus of killing innocents. The identification of authority figures with animals makes murder a simple slaughter of inferior life. The continual picture held up to group members is that there are oppressors and oppressed; they are fighting inhuman opponents in the name of the oppressed.

This is the other aspect of de-humanization. By making "the oppressed" or "the people" an abstract concept, usually an ignorant mass, it permits the individual terrorist to claim to act on their behalf. The terrorist believes these acts further the interests of some "un-awakened" social or ethnic constituency that is too oppressed or misinformed to realize its interests. They see themselves as leading the struggle on behalf of the rest of whatever constituency they represent. This view on the part of terrorists is common to all shades of the political spectrum. It is variously identified as "the revolutionary vanguard" or "true patriots," but involves the terrorists acting for the good of either a silent or ignorant mass that would approve of their struggle if they were free to choose or if they understood.

LIFESTYLE ATTRACTIONS

There's something about a good bomb.
Bill Ayers, Former Weather Underground
Leader in his memoir "Fugitive Days"

The lifestyle of a terrorist, while not particularly appealing for members of stable societies, can provide emotional, physical and sometimes social rewards. Emotional rewards include the feelings of notoriety, power, and belonging. In some societies, there may be a sense of satisfaction in rebellion; in others there may be a perceived increase in social status or power. For some, the intense sense of belonging generated by membership in an illegal group is emotionally satisfying.[6] Physical rewards can include such things as money, authority, and adventure.[7] This lure can subvert other motives. Several of the more notorious terrorists of the 1970s and 1980s, such as Abu Nidal,[8] became highly specialized mercenaries, discarding their convictions and working for a variety of causes and sponsors. Abu Nidal is a nom de guerre for Sabri al-Banna and an international terrorist group named after its founder "Abu Nidal"—Abu Nidal Organization (ANO).[9] Sabris al-Banna rose in notoriety in the Palestine Liberation Organization (PLO) but broke away from the PLO to form his own terror organization in the mid-1970s. The group's goals center on the destruction of the state of Israel, but the group has served as a mercenary terrorist force with connections to several radical regimes including Iraq, Syria, and Libya.[10] ANO activities link to terrorist attacks in 20 countries with killing about 300 people and injuring hundreds of additional people totaling estimates of about 900 victims.[11]

Lifestyle attractions also include a sense of elitism, and a feeling of freedom from societal mores. "Nothing in my life had ever been this exciting!" enthused Susan Stern, member of the Weather Underground, describing her involvement with the group.[12]

Behaviors Within Organizations

People within groups have different behaviors collectively than they do as individuals. This is as true of terrorists as it is of audiences at concerts or members of book clubs. Terrorist organizations have varying motives and reasons for existence, and how the group interprets these guides or determines internal group dynamics.

Groups are collectively more daring and ruthless than the individual members. No individual wishes to appear less committed than the others, and will not object to proposals within the group they would never entertain as an individual.[13] Leaders will not risk being seen as timid, for fear of losing their influence over the group. The end result can be actions not in keeping with individual behavior patterns as far as risk and lethality, but dictated by the pressure of group expectations and suppression of dissent and caution.

Group commitment stresses secrecy and loyalty to the group. Disagreements are discouraged by the sense of the external threat represented by the outside world, and pressure to conform to the group view. Excommunication from the group adds to the group's loathing and hatred of doubters or deserters.[14] Even the slightest suspicion of disloyalty can result in torture and murder of the suspect. The ideological intensity that makes terrorists such formidable enemies often turns upon itself, and some groups have purged themselves so effectively that they almost ceased to exist.[15] Frequently, the existence of the group becomes more important than the goal they originally embraced. If the group nears success, it will often adjust objectives so as to have a reason for continued existence. In some cases, success can mean disbanding the organization, an option to be rejected by individuals or factions whose fundamental identity and personal worth is derived from being a terrorist. Factions that advocate keeping to the original objective will inspire bitter in-fighting and schism in the group. The resulting splinter groups or dissenting individual members are extremely volatile and run the risk of compromising the original group's purpose.

In cases where the terrorists are not tied to a particular political or social goal, groups will even adopt a new cause if the original one is resolved. When first formed, many of the Euro-terror groups such as the Red Army Faction (Germany) and Communist Combatant Cells (Belgium) grew out of the 1960s student protest movement. The initial motivations for their actions were supposedly to protest U.S. involvement in Vietnam and support the North Vietnamese government. When American involvement in Vietnam came to an end, the radical left in Europe embraced Palestinian and pro-Arab causes rather than disband. Later, they conducted attacks against research facilities supporting the U.S. Strategic Defense Initiative, and to prevent deployment of the Pershing IRBM (Intermediate Range Ballistic Missile) in Germany. These examples of liberal, very left-wing viewpoints illustrate that groups can align themselves with causes in keeping with their own goals and the way they visualize group value.

Organizations that are experiencing difficulties may tend to increase their level of violence. This increase in violence can occur when frustration and low morale develops within the group due to lack of perceived progress or successful counter-terrorism measures that may limit freedom of action within the terrorist group. Members attempt to perform more effectively, but such organizational and cooperative impediments usually result in poor operational performance. The organization hopes that a change to more spectacular tactics or larger casualty lists will overcome the group's internal problems.[16] An example of this occurred in Kashmir in 2003. After an increase in suicide attacks, the chief military leader of India's northern command in Kashmir stated that militants were launching attacks to lift the morale of their cadres, because continued Indian army operations were killing six to eight militants a day, thus weakening the groups.[17]

Another example of this phenomenon is the terrorist group, al Qaeda in the Arabian Peninsula. This regional arm of al Qaeda in Saudi Arabia is one of several associated subgroups in a larger global reach terrorist organization, al Qaeda. During a 13-month period, this al Qaeda sub-group sustained a number of arrests and killings of their members, including the group's leader being killed and replaced four times. In May and June 2004, the sub-group conducted a wave of hostage taking, beheadings, and gruesome murders. An interview by *Sawt Al-Jihad*, an al Qaeda identified journal, was conducted with the commander of the Al-Quds Brigade, a subordinate unit of the group that took responsibility for the May 29, 2004 Oasis Compound attack at al-Khobar, Saudi Arabia where 22 people were killed. During this interview, the terrorist commander claimed they had either beheaded or cut the throats of more than 12 of the victims.[18] Al Qaeda in the Arabian Peninsula was also responsible for a number of other murders, including the killing of Robert Jacobs, an American employee of Vinnell Corporation, and the beheading of Paul Johnson, an American employee of Lockheed-Martin. In both of these, the terrorist group released gruesome videos of the murders.

SECTION II: IMPACT OF TERRORIST GOALS & MOTIVATIONS ON PLANNING

Practical strategies against terrorists require consideration of the terrorist's point of view in his targeting and operations. Understanding the opponents' preferences and capabilities allows better defense and promotes an active approach to the threat. Total interdiction of all possible targets is impossible, since the defender cannot protect everything. While consistent prediction is unlikely, accurate determination of what risks are acceptable must consider the terrorists' values, particularly their estimate of the target's value, and the costs of the terrorist operation necessary to successfully hit it.

The proliferation of terrorism expertise, and the breakdown in restraint and observance of international norms allow many more groups and individuals to use terror as a viable tool[19] in order to achieve their goals. With more potential terror users, the U.S. will often be a terrorist target for several reasons.

There has been an increase in transnational radicalism as compared to recent historical conflicts. As the most prominent secular democracy and largest single economic, military, and political power in the world, the

U.S. becomes an easy and appealing target for extremists. Additionally, since the United States declared the Global War on Terrorism, the U.S. has become the principal opponent of extremists throughout the world. Much of the current thinking and literature on terrorism developed when terrorism was closely tied to revolutionary movements and separatist movements concerned with influencing events in relation to one nation. Newer causes and ideologies, such as religion, economic concerns, or environmental issues are international, transnational, or even global in scope.

Further, the perception that the U.S. is the single most powerful nation in the world invites targeting by terror groups regardless of ideology to demonstrate their power and status. In the worldview of many terrorist groups, the perceived power and influence of the U.S. encourages targeting to force the U.S. to extract concessions from third parties (e.g., prisoner release, policy changes). Although some people may question why a comparatively small terrorist group believes it can successfully confront the United States, part of the answer lies in the Afghanistan jihad fighters and their success against the Soviet Union. Many of these Islamic fighters were persuaded that they alone had defeated the Soviet Union in Afghanistan (even though the U.S. provided substantial support) and that they could do the same to the United States.[20]

Another reason to expect greater use of terrorism against the U.S. is that possible competitors may feel that they cannot openly challenge or defeat the U.S. with any other technique. Nations have employed state sponsored terrorism to produce results that could not have otherwise been achieved against U.S. opposition. The current supremacy of American military power leaves adversaries with few options to challenge U.S. interests. Adding non-state groups of formidable capability and few restraints to the roster of potential adversaries of the U.S. increases the likely use of terror against our forces.

Many potential adversaries view the U.S. as particularly vulnerable to the psychological impact and uncertainties generated by terror tactics in support of other activities.[21] Terrorism and terror tactics have already been used against U.S. forces in support of conventional and insurgent warfare, as well as against U.S. forces during stability and peace support operations in attempts to influence policy.

> *We are an instrument for the hostages… We force the*
> *Administration to put their lives above policy.*
>> Lesley Stahl, CBS White House correspondent
>> during the TWA flight 847 hostage crisis, 1985

support for harsh and undemocratic governments results in the exportation of essentially national resistance movements. Thus, when Americans wonder why they are targeted, they might take a look at the company their leaders keep.

NOTES

* "Mujahid Usamah bin Ladin Talks Exclusively to 'Nidal 'Ul Islam' About the New Powder Keg in the Middle East," *Nida'ul Islam* 15 (October/November 1996). Available online, http://www.fas.org/irp/world/para/docs/LADIN.htm (accessed December 7, 2006).

Why America?
The Globalization of Civil War
MARTHA CRENSHAW

The magnitude of the September 11 assaults on the World Trade Center and the Pentagon was unprecedented in the history of terrorism. The method of attack represented a novel combination of the familiar tactics of aircraft hijackings, which began in 1968, and suicide bombings, which developed in the 1980s. The four simultaneous hijackings required much more complicated and long-term planning and organization than had previous terrorist actions. Subsequent investigations revealed the existence of a vast and complex transnational conspiracy behind the hijackings.

The September 11 attacks are also the culmination of a pattern of anti-American terrorism on the international level. Since the late 1960s the United States has been a preferred target, the victim of approximately one-third of all international terrorist attacks over the past 30 years. In most instances Americans and American interests were attractive to the practitioners of terrorism because of United States support for unpopular local governments or regional enemies. This terrorism can thus be interpreted as a form of compellence: the use or threat of violence to compel the United States to withdraw from its external commitments. Terrorism should be seen as a strategic reaction to American power in the context of globalized civil war. Extremist religious beliefs play a role in motivating terrorism, but they also display an instrumental logic.

MAKING THE UNITED STATES THE TARGET

The development of international terrorism as it came to characterize the second half of the twentieth century was initially associated with left-wing social revolution. Beginning in 1965, the war in Vietnam legitimized anti-Americanism and equated hostility to the United States with anti-imperialism and national liberation around the world. Independent terrorist campaigns also emerged simultaneously in Latin America, the Middle East, and Europe as a result of localized conflicts and issues. These converging waves of terrorism shared an important feature that distinguished them from earlier violence. Primarily, the attacks involved the seizure of hostages to make political demands on governments. They also involved attacks on diplomats and on civil aviation, a newly available and convenient target.

In Central and South America, kidnappings and assassinations of American and other Western diplomats broke the taboo of diplomatic immunity. Revolutionary organizations, typically inspired by the Cuban example, wanted to demonstrate American complicity in perpetuating the military dictatorships they sought to overthrow. Their belief was that if the dependence of authoritarian regimes on superior outside power could either be revealed to the world or brought to an end, revolution could succeed. Unable to mobilize the countryside, their strategic emphasis shifted from rural insurgency to "urban guerrilla" warfare. Violent revolutionary campaigns flared briefly but were suppressed, often with extreme brutality, in the late 1960s and 1970s.

In the Middle East, the stunning Arab defeat in the 1967 Arab-Israeli war and the Israeli occupation of the West Bank and the Gaza Strip aroused a Palestinian national consciousness. To the newly established Palestine Liberation Organization (PLO) under the leadership of Yasir Arafat, the unmistakable lesson was that neither conventional war nor reliance on sympathetic Arab states could help the Palestinian cause. In 1968 the Popular Front for the Liberation of Palestine (PFLP), a minority faction of the PLO, initiated the practice of hijackings by seizing an Israeli El Al airliner. The PFLP claimed that the airplane was a legitimate military target because El Al had been used to transport Israeli troops in 1967.

The strategy quickly expanded to include the airlines of any country dealing with Israel—including the United States, which was fast becoming Israel's chief ally and weapons supplier. In 1970 the PFLP accomplished a feat that before September 2001 was considered, according to analyst Peter St. John, the "most dramatic multiple hijack in history." A TWA plane from Frankfurt, a Swissair flight from Zurich, and an El Al flight from New York were hijacked to Jordan on September 6. At the same time, a Pan Am plane was hijacked to Cairo. Two days later, a British plane was also hijacked. Four of the planes were destroyed. Fortunately, the hundreds of passengers were eventually released unharmed.

Terrorism generated by the conflict between Israel and the Palestinians escalated to include not only hijackings that ended without loss of life but also lethal attacks on diplomats, takeovers of embassies or other prominent public buildings ("barricade and hostage" incidents), bombings of aircraft, and armed attacks on passengers at airports. Most terrorist incidents were attributable to the more radical and Marxist-oriented Palestinian factions, which also attacked conservative Arab regimes. (As in Latin America, these regimes were doubly vulnerable as local elites and as American allies.) These secular extremist groups aimed for revolution throughout the Arab world, not just the liberation of Palestine.

Also as in Latin America, Middle Eastern terrorism involved attacks on diplomatic targets, notably in the March 1973 Khartoum incident in Sudan. Two American diplomats and a Belgian diplomat were killed by the Palestinian Black September organization, which had seized the Saudi Arabian embassy during a diplomatic reception. The American rejection of the hostage-takers' demands marked the first implementation of the recently adopted no-concessions policy. Subsequent terrorist attacks killed American passengers at the Rome and Athens airports in August and December. In 1974 a TWA plane en route from Tel Aviv to New York crashed as a result of an on-board explosion, for which the Arab Nationalist Youth for the Liberation of Palestine took credit. In 1976 PFLP militants assassinated the American ambassador to Lebanon, along with the embassy's economic counselor.

Membership in NATO as well as the Vietnam war enhanced the attractiveness of American targets in Western Europe, where two related developments stimulated terrorism. First, indigenous left-revolutionary movements rose from social protest movements in West Germany and Italy. Their roots were primarily in student disaffection, framed in terms of anti-imperialism and sympathy for the third world. Second, although the social and political roots of these organizations were domestic rather than international, they were inspired and assisted by the spillover of Palestinian terrorism to the European scene. This spillover effect was demonstrated most shockingly with the Black September attack on Israeli athletes at the 1972 Munich Olympics, during which 11 Israeli athletes were killed. Combined operations between German and Palestinian groups became reasonably common in the 1970s, as did cooperation between Palestinians and the Japanese Red Army.

Furthermore, West European revolutionaries, lacking popular support, saw their mission not only as overthrowing oppressive regimes at home but as assisting third world revolutionary movements, protesting American involvement in the Vietnam war, and revealing that NATO's European members were merely fascist puppets of American hegemonic ambitions. The American military presence was thus anathema, leading to bombings of military bases (especially air force bases in Germany), assassination attempts, and kidnappings (for example, of General James Dozier in Italy in 1980).[1] Terrorism in Western Europe declined through the 1980s as governments became more efficient at countering the problem and as the social movements from which the terrorist groups recruited subsided.

ENTER THE STATE—AND RELIGION

In the 1980s, terrorism did not end but shifted course. Persistent state involvement, or "sponsorship," of terrorism, especially by Libya and Iran, marked this period. The decade saw the advent of what is thought of as religious terrorism, driven by the success of the Iran's Islamic revolution in 1979 and Iran's intervention in the Lebanese civil war on the side of Lebanon's Shia community in the 1980s. The war between Iran and Iraq that began in September 1980 exacerbated tensions between Iran and the West, since most Western states sided with Iraq. Libya supported anti-American terrorism for reasons that remain obscure beyond a generic anti-imperialism without religious connotations.

The administration of President Ronald Reagan immediately adopted a "proactive" stance toward terrorism. The Iran hostage crisis had been a major turning point for the United States and a painful personal defeat for the previous president, Jimmy Carter. The crisis had a profound impact for several reasons: the Iranian government's public assumption of responsibility for seizing and holding American diplomats; the seriousness of the violation of international laws and norms; and the apparent success of state terrorism. The failed military mission to rescue the embassy hostages was an added blow to American prestige. The Reagan administration was determined to respond vigorously to the next challenge.

The hostage crisis reverberated beyond the immediate Iranian context not only because of the lessons learned by the United States but also because Iran was determined to spread the Islamic revolution to surrounding Arab countries with Shiite populations: from Lebanon and Iraq to American allies such as Kuwait. Iranian ambitions thus threatened the stability of a region that was and is economically and strategically vital to

In 1997, from his hidden bases in the caves of Afghanistan, bin Laden gave an interview to CNN in which he declared a jihad against the United States. He had issued earlier calls to arms but now used American television media to communicate his message. He claimed that jihad was a response to United States support for Israel, America's military presence in Saudi Arabia, and America's "aggressive intervention against Muslims in the whole world." In 1998 he joined with Egyptian Islamic Jihad to establish an "International Front for Islamic Holy War against the Jews and Crusaders." The front called for attacks on American targets across the globe, both civil and military, to force an American withdrawal from Saudi Arabia and to end the Israeli occupation of Jerusalem. It focused on the plight of the Iraqi people, but not the Palestinian cause. This appeal was ambitiously presented as a *fatwa*, or religious edict, which all Muslims were called on to obey.

In 1996 the United States had already initiated a grand jury investigation into bin Laden's activities, and the CIA began to target and "disrupt" his network. By the spring United States agencies were specifically monitoring his activities in Nairobi, Kenya. In March 1998 the State Department issued a worldwide alert drawing attention to a threat against American military and civilians following the February *fatwa*. A sealed indictment in June 1998 led to the arrest of 21 of bin Laden's associates during the summer. It charged the group with attacks on United States and UN troops in Somalia in 1993 and with leading a terrorist conspiracy in concert with Sudan, Iraq, and Iran. Press reports later indicated that the United States was also considering a raid into Afghanistan to arrest bin Laden, as a result of a 1998 presidential finding that authorized covert operations, including blocking bin Laden's financial assets and exercising close surveillance.

Despite this awareness and these actions, the August 1998 bombings of the American embassies in Kenya and Tanzania came as a surprise. The Nairobi bombing killed 12 Americans, 32 other United States employees, and more than 200 Kenyans. Thousands were injured. In Dar es Salaam, Tanzania, 11 people were killed and 85 injured. No Americans died. In form, the attacks resembled the bombings of the United States embassy in Beirut in 1983 and 1984, but the message was not that the United States should withdraw from Kenya and Tanzania. The intent instead appeared to be to issue a general warning of a terrorist campaign. In tactical terms, what distinguished the attacks and alarmed American authorities was that two embassies in different countries were bombed simultaneously, which indicated a highly organized conspiracy.

The Clinton administration responded immediately with cruise missile attacks on Al Qaeda training camps in Afghanistan and on a pharmaceuticals plant in the Sudan. (The latter was suspected of man-ufacturing precursor chemicals for weapons use and was believed to have connections to bin Laden's business enterprises as well as to the Sudanese regime.) The decision to use military force was controversial. In particular, critics disputed the link between the pharmaceuticals plant, chemical precursors, and bin Laden. The retaliatory attacks may have been a signal of American resolve, but they inflicted no serious damage on Al Qaeda's capabilities. They may also have cost the United States the moral high ground. Rather than stressing that most of the victims of the bombings were African, the United States was seen to be bombing Muslim countries.

A second avenue of response was a strengthened law enforcement effort. United States authorities quickly apprehended four of the men who planned and executed the East Africa bombings. All four were con-victed (and in October 2001 they were sentenced to life in prison). The group included a Saudi, a Tanzanian, a Jordanian, and an American who was born in Lebanon. Two were charged with direct participation; the other two were found guilty of participation in the broader conspiracy. The lengthy trial in New York revealed many details of the operations of the Al Qaeda network, which appeared less like a cult of religious zealots than a far-reaching and profitable business enterprise. Bin Laden was said to control a global banking network as well as agricultural, construc-tion, transportation, and investment companies in Sudan. Bin Laden was also said to have developed his hostility to the United States as a result of the 1993 intervention in Somalia. According to witness testimony (from Jamal Ahmed al-Fadl, a former bin Laden associate who had been cooperating with the United States since 1996), Al Qaeda was divided over whether to retaliate after the arrest of Sheik Rahman in 1993. The Egyptian members wanted to avenge his arrest, but others objected that innocent people would be killed. Some of the Egyptian members then left the organization.

The Taliban continued to reject the American demand to surrender bin Laden, which was first made in 1998. This persistent refusal resulted in the imposition of United Nations sanctions and the isolation of the Taliban regime.

The next public manifestation of Al Qaeda's terrorist activity came in December 1999, when a series of "millennium plots" was foiled. One involved an Algerian, Ahmed Ressam, who entered the United States from Canada to bomb the Los Angeles airport. His fortuitous arrest showed that Al Qaeda cells were operating in Canada and that the Algerian Armed Islamic Group (GIA) was involved. The plot was also linked to Al Qaeda cells in Britain. Eventually four Algerians were charged in the plot and brought to trial in June and July 2001.

Training in Afghanistan was a common theme in their experience. Ahmed Ressam described a decentralized organizational structure. Militants were trained by the organization, but then given funds and substantial autonomy in selecting targets. He also testified that Sheik Rahman had issued orders to kill Americans. (Another thwarted millennium plot involved attacks on tourists in Jordan and Israel. Jordan arrested a number of suspects.)

The link between Al Qaeda and the GIA was a product of Algeria's bloody civil war in the 1990s. When the Islamic Salvation Front was poised to win Algeria's national elections in December 1991, the Algerian government canceled the results. The GIA emerged as the most extreme of the opposition movements. In 1994 members of the GIA hijacked a plane to Marseilles and threatened to fly it into the Eiffel Tower before they were killed by French security forces. As elsewhere, many Algerian militants had fought in Afghanistan in the 1980s.

In October 2000 Al Qaeda struck again. Although conclusive proof is lacking, the United States is certain that bin Laden's followers organized the suicide bombing of the United States destroyer *Cole* while it was refueling in Yemen. The death toll was 17 Navy personnel. The bombers were apparently Yemenis, but bin Laden was suspected of backing them. The mastermind was thought to be a Saudi of Yemeni origin, living in the United Arab Emirates. As in Saudi Arabia, the FBI encountered difficulties in getting Yemeni authorities to cooperate in the investigation.

THE SCOPE BROADENS

The attacks of September 11 fit a pattern but also marked a dramatic escalation of violence. Subsequent investigations into the hijackings also revealed the astonishing scope of the transnational conspiracy involved. The hijackers included Egyptian, Saudi, and Lebanese citizens. The apparent leaders came from a cell headquartered at a technical university in Hamburg, Germany. Arrests in other countries such as Spain, Britain, Germany, and France targeted Kuwaiti, French, Algerian, Yemeni, Moroccan, Libyan, Syrian, and Tunisian activists, among others. One group was apparently organizing a parallel plot to attack the American embassy in Paris. The organizers were mostly Al Qaeda second-generation Algerians in France. The European branch of the conspiracy was said to revolve around two groups, the Egyptian Takfir wal Hijra (known in Europe as Vanguards of the Conquest or the New Jihad Group), led by Al Qaeda lieutenant Ayman al-Zawahiri, and the Algerian Salafist Group for Preaching and Combat. The Salafists are thought to work with bin Laden but to maintain an independent leadership (in 1998 the Salafist Group broke from the GIA and apparently formed an alliance with Al Qaeda).

The reasoning behind the September 11 attacks was expressed primarily in a statement from bin Laden broadcast in Qatar on October 7, and to a lesser degree in subsequent pronouncements from Al Qaeda leaders. Such statements show a keen appreciation of different audiences and constituencies and are attuned to sensitivities to specific grievances. Typically, bin Laden did not claim direct credit for the actions but praised those responsible as a "group of vanguard Muslims." The statement referred specifically to 80 years of humiliation of Islam. It thus apparently dated the period of humiliation to 1921, the dissolution of the Ottoman Empire, and the establishment of Britain's Palestine Mandate that provided for a Jewish homeland. Specific references to Palestine and Iraq were made, as well as more vague allegations that countries that believe in Islam had been turned against bin Laden by the United States. Bin Laden cited United States retaliation against Afghanistan in 1998 as another grievance. Echoing Ramzi Yousef, he also condemned the United States bombing of Japan in 1945. This comparison may be an attempt to provide moral justification for causing large numbers of civilian casualties.

The anthrax incidents this October have not been conclusively linked to Al Qaeda operatives. Previously, the only terrorist attacks using chemical and biological weapons occurred in Japan, most notably with the subway sarin gas attack in 1995 by the Aum Shinrikyo cult. Since then the American government had undertaken a range of efforts to protect American cities and prepare for terrorist-caused disaster ("consequence management"). "Bioterrorism" was seen as the most likely manifestation of the threat. Even if the anthrax scare is not linked to international terrorism, it will increase fears that such attacks are likely.

THE PREPOSTEROUS IDEA

The United States has been susceptible to international terrorism primarily because of its engagement on the world scene and its choice of allies. Extremist groups in countries around the world have targeted United States interests in an effort to achieve radical political change at home. The United States military presence, whether in assisting local regimes or in peacemaking exercises, attracted terrorism, but so too did diplomatic and cultural institutions.

In the 1990s, a determined leadership, drawing its inspiration from an extreme version of Islam, took advantage of permissive political conditions and ample financial resources to construct a transnational terrorist coalition with deadly ambitions. To Americans, the idea that the United States could be compelled by terrorism to abandon its interests in the Middle East is preposterous; to the leaders and followers of Al Qaeda there is precedent in Lebanon and Somalia. In a war of attrition, superior motivation is often the key to the successful compellence of an adversary, and terrorism is a way of demonstrating their determination and power. When civil war is expanded to the international system, vulnerability may be the inevitable accompaniment to the exercise of power. Although the response must deal with the immediate threat and the actors who are behind it, it must also deal with the long term. Future American foreign policy must consider the risk of terrorism as a central factor in calculating interests and strategies.

NOTES

1. The United States experienced a similar domestic phenomenon, growing out of the student protest movement. However, the Weather Underground collapsed in the early stages of violence.

2. For a discussion of the general problem as well as specific accounts of Egypt and Algeria, see Fawaz A. Gerges, *America and Political Islam: Clash of Cultures or Clash of Interests?* (Cambridge: Cambridge University Press, 1999).

Reprinted with permission from *Current History* magazine (December 2001). © 2007 Current History, Inc.

Bibliography

———— ⊸∞⊷ ————

SECTION ONE: WHO ARE THESE TERRORISTS?

Stern, Jessica. "The Protean Enemy." *Foreign Affairs* 82, no. 4 (July/August 2003): 27–40.

"Terrorist Behaviors, Motivations, and Characteristics." In *A Military Guide to Terrorism in the Twenty-First Century*, 64–67. Fort Leavenworth, Kans.: U.S. Army Training and Doctrine Command, 2005.

Sprinzak, Ehud. "The Lone Gunman." *Foreign Policy* (November/December 2001): 72–73.

SECTION TWO: WHAT EXACTLY IS TERRORISM?

Hoffman, Bruce. "Distinctions as a Path to Definition," from *Inside Terrorism*. New York: Columbia University Press, 1998, 41–44.

Juergensmeyer, Mark. "Understanding the New Terrorism." *Current History* 99, no. 636 (April 2000): 158–163.

Laqueur, Walter. "Postmodern Terrorism." *Foreign Affairs* 75, no. 5 (September/October 1996): 24–36.

Pressmen, Jeremy. "Leaderless Resistance: The Next Threat?" *Current History* 102, no. 668 (December 2003): 422–425.

SECTION THREE: HOW LONG HAS TERRORISM BEEN AROUND?

Laqueur, Walter. "Terrorism and History" from *The New Terrorism: Fanaticism and the Arms of Mass Destruction*. New York: Oxford University Press, 1999, 8–36.

Rapoport, David C. "The Fourth Wave: September 11 in the History of Terrorism." *Current History* 100, no. 650 (December 2001): 419–424.

SECTION FOUR: WHERE DO TERRORISTS COME FROM?

Bergen, Peter, and Alec Reynolds. "Blowback Revisited: Today's Insurgents in Iraq Are Tomorrow's Terrorists." *Foreign Affairs* 84, no. 6 (November/December 2005): 2–6.

Evans, Alexander. "Understanding Madrasahs: How Threatening Are They?" *Foreign Affairs* 85, no. 1 (January/February 2006):9–16.

SECTION FIVE: WHAT WEAPONS DO TERRORISTS HAVE?

Cameron, Gavin. "Nuclear Terrorism Reconsidered." *Current History* 99, no. 636 (April 2000): 154–157.

Conway, Maura. "What is Cyberterrorism?" *Current History* (December 2002): 436–442.

Luft, Gal and Anne Korin. "Terrorism Goes to Sea." *Foreign Affairs* 83, no. 6 (November/December 2004): 61–71.

Tucker, Jonathan B. "Chemical and Biological Terrorism: How Real a Threat?" *Current History* 99, no. 636 (April 2000): 147–153.

SECTION SIX: WHY DO THEY DO IT?

Crenshaw, Martha. "Why America? The Globalization of Civil War." *Current History* 100, no. 650 (December 2001): 425–432.

"Terrorist Behaviors, Motivations, and Characteristics." In *A Military Guide to Terrorism in the Twenty-First Century*, 53–64. Fort Leavenworth, Kans.: U.S. Army Training and Doctrine Command, 2005.

Sources Cited

Burnett, John S. *Dangerous Waters: Modern Piracy and Terror on the High Seas.* New York: Dutton, 2002.

Carr, Caleb. *The Lessons of Terror: A History of Warfare Against Civilians.* New York: Random House, 2003.

Crenshaw, Martha. "The Logic of Terrorism: Terrorist Behavior as a Product of Strategic Choice." In *Origins Of Terror: Psychologies,*

Ideologies, Theologies, States of Mind, edited by Walter Reich. Washington, D.C.: Woodrow Wilson Center Press, 1998.

Cronin, Isaac. *Confronting Fear: A History of Terrorism.* New York: Thunder's Mouth Press, 2002.

Davies, Barry *Terrorism: Inside a World Phenomenon.* London: Virgin Books, 2003.

Fraser, Steve. "Crowds and Power." Review of *Death in the Haymarket: A Story of Chicago, the First Labor Movement, and the Bombing that Divided Gilded Age America,* by James Green. *The Nation* (April 2006).

Lipton, Eric. "Report Sees Confusion Likely in a Sea Attack by Terrorists." *New York Times,* April 4, 2006, A17.

Lynn, John A. *Battle: A History of Combat and Culture.* Cambridge, Mass.: Westview Press, 2004.

Simonsen, Clifford E., and Jeremy R. Spindlove, eds., *Terrorism Today: The Past, The Players, The Future.* Upper Saddle River, N.J.: Prentice Hall, 1999.

Web Content

"Al Qaeda Training Manual, Military Series." Available online. URL: http://www.fas.org/irp/world/para/manualpart1_1.pdf (accessed December 7, 2006).

Allison, Graham "How to Stop Nuclear Terror," *Foreign Affairs* (January/February 2004). Available online. URL: http://www.foreignaffairs .org/20040101faessay83107/graham-allison/how-to-stop-nuclear-terror.html (accessed December 7, 2006).

Katzman, Kenneth. "Al Qaeda: Profile and Threat Assessment." *Congressional Research Service, Library of Congress* (August 2005). Available online. URL: http://www.fas.org/sgp/crs/terror/RL33038 .pdf (accessed December 7, 2006).

"Mujahid Usamah bin Ladin Talks Exclusively to 'Nidal 'Ul Islam' About the New Powder Keg in the Middle East." *Nida'ul Islam* 15 (October/November 1996). Available online. URL: http://www.fas.org/irp/world/para/docs/LADIN.htm (accessed December 7, 2006).

Further Reading

Books

Barnaby, Frank. *How to Build a Nuclear Bomb—and Other Weapons of Mass Destruction*. New York: Nation Books, 2004.

Bloom, Mia. *Dying to Kill: The Allure of Suicide Terror*. New York: Columbia University Press, 2005.

Marquette, Scott. *America Under Attack*. Vero Beach, Florida: Rourke Publishing, 2003.

McCuen, Gary E. *Biological Terrorism and Weapons of Mass Destruction*. Hudson, Wisconsin: McCuen Publications, 1999.

Nacos, Brigette Lebens. *Mass-Mediated Terrorism: The Central Role of the Media in Terrorism and Counterterrorism*. Lanham, Maryland: Rowman and Littlefield, 2002.

Nassar, Jamal R. *Globalization and Terrorism: The Migration of Dreams and Nightmares*. Lanham, Maryland: Rowman and Littlefield, 2005.

Williams, Paul. *Al Qaeda: Brotherhood of Terror*. New York: Alpha Books, 2002.

Web sites

Council on Foreign Relations: Terrorism. Online at http://www.cfr.org/issue/135/.

Central Intelligence Agency: The War on Terrorism. Online at http://www.cia.gov/terrorism/.

MIPT Terrorism Knowledge Base. Online at http://www.tkb.org/Home.jsp.

Naval Post-Graduate School: Terrorism. Online at http://library.nps.navy.mil/home/terrorism.htm.

Terrorism Research Center. Online at
http://www.terrorism.com/.

FAS—Intelligence Resource program. Online at
http://www.fas.org/irp/world/para/ladin.htm.

Index

A

Abdel Rahman, Omar, 120
abortion, 61–62
Abouhalima, Mahmud, 58–60
Abu Nidal, 185, 202
Abu Sayyaf, 26, 121
Achille Lauro, 202
adaptability, 23–33
Afghanistan, 49, 54, 111, 119–122, 203–204, 206–209
age, terrorists and, 16–17
airplane hijackings. *See* hijackings
al Qaeda
    Afghanistan and, 120–121
    education and, 127
    Egypt and, 205
    fourth wave of terrorism and, 115
    group mentality and, 187
    modern methodology of, 32–33
    motivations of, 24–26, 111, 204–205
    networking and, 26–29, 54, 176
    nuclear weapons and, 160
    ocean terrorism and, 138–139
    oil terrorism and, 140–141
    organized crime and, 29–32
    plans of for future, 23
    secrecy and, 48–55
al-Banna, Sabris, 185
Aleph. *See* Aum Shinrikyo
Alexander II (Tsar of Russia), 82–84
alliances, 26–28, 196–200, 203–209
Amir, Yigal, 20, 21, 39–40
anarchists, 79, 81, 112
anthrax, 148–149, 156, 210
apocalypse, 43–44, 62–63, 149
Argentina, 91–92

Armed Islamic Group (GIA), 120, 121, 171, 208–209, 210
Asahara, Shoko, 20, 43, 62–63
assassinations, 36–37, 39–40, 70, 82–87, 90–91, 112
Assassins, 76–77, 78, 110
Atta, Muhammad, 30
Aum Shinrikyo
    fanaticism of, 43, 62–63
    performance violence and, 60
    weapons of, 41, 147–148, 151–152, 154–155, 160

B

Baader Meinhof group, 94–95, 97, 121, 186, 199
bases of terrorism, identification of, 118–124
Basque Homeland and Liberty (ETA) movement, 38, 40, 99, 101–102, 163, 172
bin Laden, Osama, 16, 20, 25, 120–121, 205, 206–209
biological weapons, 32, 40–41, 146–157
blowback, 119–124
brain drain, 155–156
Branch Davidian sect, 61–62, 67
Bray, Michael, 61–62, 67
Brazil, 92–93
Brzezinski, Zbigniew, 124

C

Carmichael, Stokley, 96–97
Carnot, Sadi, 37
Cavendish (Lord), 82–83
Chaos International, 44
Chávez, Hugo, 27

About the Editor

―――∞∞∞――――

JOHN C. DAVENPORT holds a Ph.D. from the University of Connecticut and currently teaches at Corte Madera School in Portola Valley, California. Davenport is the author of several biographies, including one of Muslim leader Saladin, and has written extensively on the role of borders in American history. He lives in San Carlos, California, with his wife, Jennifer, and his two sons, William and Andrew.

Photo Credits

―――∞∞∞――――

PAGE

    13:   Getty Images
    35:   © Greg Smith/Corbis
    73:   Library of Congress
  117:   Department of Defense
  135:   Department of Defense
  179:   © Rob Howard/Corbis

  cover: Associated Press, AP